KV-354-584

CONTENTS

Foreword

A FEAST OF WORDS

A FEAST OF WORDS

*An anthology for exploring
Christian worship*

Leslie J Francis
and Nicola M Slee

COLLINS

Collins Liturgical Publications
187 Piccadilly, London W1V 9DA

Collins Liturgical Australia
55 Clarence St Sydney 2000 PO Box 3023 Sydney 2001

ISBN 0 00 599736 4
© compilation 1983 Leslie J. Francis and Nicola M. Slee
First published 1983

Photograph credits:
W. Cribbin, p. 52
C. Horsman, p. 19
Carlos Reyes, pp. 2, 8, 26, 33, 43, 49, 60, 68, 72, 74, 79, 90, Cover

Typographical design by Colin Reed
Phototypesetting by Rowland Phototypesetting
Bury St Edmunds, Suffolk
Printed in Great Britain by
William Collins Sons & Co Ltd, Glasgow

FOREWORD

In Christian worship a certain number of key themes and images continually recur. These themes and images have their roots in the world around us and in the common experience of men and women. They take on religious meaning when they are incorporated into the life of the Christian Church, in prayer, scripture, liturgy, creed and sacrament.

This anthology selects just four of these key themes – meetings, water, mystery and music. These themes are explored from a variety of perspectives in order to highlight the richness and diversity of the language of Christian worship.

The extracts used are drawn from a wide range of sources, including fiction, biography, poetry, journalism, scripture, liturgy, theology, prayer and meditation. They have been selected and arranged to appeal to personal experience, develop powers of imagination and extend the capacity for deep reflection.

The anthology has been designed for two kinds of readers. First, it will help those who are not members of a Christian church to understand more fully the sort of language which Christian believers use in their worship. In this sense the anthology will be of help to those studying Christianity in a secular school. Suggested topics for discussion and classroom activities are provided in the first appendix.

Second, it will help church members to enter more fully into the richness of the Church's liturgy. In this sense the anthology can be used in association with Leslie Francis' *His Spirit is with Us* to provide an all-age project approach to Christian nurture based on the communion service. Suggested collects and readings for use in the celebration of communion are provided in the second appendix.

A number of people have been of help to us in the design of this anthology. We owe a particular debt of gratitude to Sue Chapman, John Greer and Jo Jones, and to Carole Boorman, Clare Gowing and Heather Knight who typed various drafts of the manuscript.

Leslie J Francis   Nicola M Slee
North Cerney Rectory   Selwyn College Cambridge

November 1982

1
MEETINGS AND ENCOUNTERS

Look at your life: see how it is made up of meeting other people: family, friends, acquaintances, strangers. Each meeting is different – consider how these meetings affect your life.

Look at your life: what happens when you meet someone? Do you listen to the other person? Do you understand what that person thinks or feels? Do you want to show who you really are to that person? Do you, in fact, encounter that person? Or do you brush past without ever truly meeting?

Look at your life, says the Christian. Think of the meetings that mean most to you and which speak to you deeply. Think of the meetings with people who really understand you, who seem to know you completely. You trust them: you open your life to them. You encounter each other in depth. Your life is changed by the meeting. Meeting with God is like that.

Meetings: what do they mean?

These four poems each describe a meeting. Then they look below the surface to the deeper meaning of what was taking place.

1   There was something I wanted to say to you,
But I've forgotten.
Anyway it's been a lovely evening.
It was good just to sit and watch the fire,
To chat and ruffle our feet in the sheepskin rug.
And the coffee and buns, that was nice,
Too.

Yes, that's what I say.
It's so nice not to have to
Think
About anything.

I'll show you to the door.
Now mind the steps.
I'm afraid it's very dark out there.

I remember now
What I wanted to say.
A question it was.
I meant to ask her why she came.

Mig Holder, 'Question'

2   Words, words, words,
Words, words, words,
Can I listen past your words
And hear the song you're singing to me?

It seems like we've been talking for so many years
But I haven't heard a single thing you've said:
Is it that we don't quite know how we want to say it
Or that we aren't sure what we want to say?

Words, words, words. . . .

Sometimes I'm not sure what your words can really do.
Do they make a bridge between us or a wall?
I've got to find the spaces that are left between your words
And look in there for what you really are.

Words, words, words. . . .

I wish that there were some way to tell what you really mean
From the rest of what you merely say:
Perhaps if we could stop a while and listen quietly
We'd hear so much of what we couldn't say.

Kathy, 'Words'

3   I saw you walking as I rounded the corner:
Your face as always
That perfectly conceived citadel
A master mason's pride
But grimly practical
Defending your heart.

I thought, dully, that you would ignore me:
But you turned half back
And stopped.

'Hullo', I cried and smiled at you,
Launching a weak attack against those towering walls
And shocked
Myself
And you
By tumbling through them.

Vivienne Stapley, 'To L'

4   one winter afternoon

(at the magical hour
when is becomes if)

a bespangled clown
standing on eighth street
handed me a flower.

Nobody, it's safe
to say, observed him but

myself; and why? because

without any doubt he was
whatever (first and last)

mostpeople fear most:
a mystery for which i've
no word except alive

– that is, completely alert
and miraculously whole;

with not merely a mind and a heart

but unquestionably a soul –
by no means funereally hilarious

(or otherwise democratic)
but essentially poetic
or ethereally serious:

a fine not a coarse clown
(no mob, but a person)

and while never saying a word

who was anything but dumb;
since the silence of him

self sang like a bird.
Mostpeople have been heard
screaming for international

measures that render hell rational
– i thank heaven somebody's crazy

enough to give me a daisy

e.e. cummings

A first meeting

First meetings and first impressions are not always what they seem. Sheldon Vanauken describes his first meeting with the girl he later marries (no. 5). Then the Old Testament tells of the first meeting between Ruth, a young foreign widow, and the well-to-do Boaz. Later they too marry (no. 6).

5   We met angrily in the dead of winter. I wanted my money back. Her job was to keep me from getting it. The scene was the photographic studio of a department store. I was probably cold and polite. She was charming but annoyed with me. She, in fact, won. On the counter between us lay a tinted miniature that had been badly done, though not by her. She, indeed, was an expert and would do it right. I left it with her and, quite possibly, stalked away.

I was then in my third year of college, home for the Christmas holidays. The miniature was of a room mate at my school, years before, who had been drowned. I wondered why I had let myself be persuaded by her. Without perceiving that I was answering the question, I remembered her quite beautiful, wide-spaced eyes, snapping with anger. . . .

I drove home, about twenty miles, still thinking of her, sometimes crossly, sometimes not. That afternoon a friend, Don . . . rang up. . . . One of our close friends, Bob, was over at college, working and alone in the House. Why didn't we, with some girls, . . . drive over? If Don had rung up a day later – or of course a day earlier – my sudden inspiration might not have come: now I thought rapidly of that girl's lovely if angry eyes. And I had her name on a receipt somewhere, didn't I? Yes, here it was: Jean Davis. And Don would be taking Margery, who just happened to be the personnel manager of that store, wouldn't he? Ah, good. Listen, Don: something I'd like you to do. Ring up Margery like a good chap and ask her to arrange. . . .

Thus it came about that on a mid-December night . . . I arrived in front of the white-columned House at the university where dwelt the lady of the angry eyes.

from Sheldon Vanauken, *A Severe Mercy*

6   Now Naomi had a kinsman on her husband's side, a
         well-to-do man of the family of Elimelech; his name was
Boaz. Ruth the Moabitess said to Naomi, 'May I go out to the
cornfields and glean behind anyone who will grant me that
favour?' 'Yes, go, my daughter', she replied. So Ruth went
gleaning in the fields behind the reapers.

As it happened, she was in that strip of the fields which
belonged to Boaz of Elimelech's family, and there was Boaz
coming out from Bethlehem. He greeted the reapers, saying,
'The Lord be with you'; and they replied, 'The Lord bless you.'
Then he asked his servant in charge of the reapers, 'Whose girl
is this?' 'She is a Moabite girl', the servant answered, 'who has
just come back with Naomi from the Moabite country. She asked
if she might glean and gather among the swathes behind the
reapers. She came and has been on her feet with hardly a
moment's rest from daybreak till now.'

Then Boaz said to Ruth, 'Listen to me, my daughter: do not go
and glean in any other field, and do not look any further, but
keep close to my girls. Watch where the men reap, and follow the
gleaners; I have given them orders not to molest you. If you are
thirsty, go and drink from the jars the men have filled.' She fell
prostrate before him and said, 'Why are you so kind as to take
notice of me when I am only a foreigner?' Boaz answered, 'They
have told me all that you have done for your mother-in-law since
your husband's death, how you left your father and mother and
the land of your birth, and came to a people you did not know
before. The Lord reward your deed; may the Lord the God of
Israel, under whose wings you have come to take refuge, give
you all that you deserve.'

Ruth 2: 1–12

Difficult Meetings

Uncertainties and doubts can make meetings difficult. These difficulties
are illustrated by Alice's meeting with Humpty Dumpty (no. 7), Nadine's
meeting with her mother-in-law (no. 8), and Norman Habel's meeting with
God (no. 9).

7   Humpty Dumpty was sitting with his legs crossed . . . on
         the top of a high wall – such a narrow one that Alice

quite wondered how he could keep his balance – and, as his eyes were steadily fixed in the opposite direction, and he didn't take the least notice of her, she thought he must be a stuffed figure after all.

'And how exactly like an egg he is!' she said aloud. . . .

'It's *very* provoking,' Humpty Dumpty said after a long silence, looking away from Alice as he spoke, 'to be called an egg – *very*!'

'I said you *looked* like an egg, Sir,' Alice gently explained. 'And some eggs are very pretty, you know,' she added, hoping to turn her remark into a sort of compliment.

'Some people,' said Humpty Dumpty, looking away from her as usual, 'have no more sense than a baby!'

Alice didn't know what to say to this: it wasn't at all like conversation, she thought, as he never said anything to *her*; in fact, his last remark was evidently addressed to a tree – so she stood and softly repeated to herself:

> 'Humpty Dumpty sat on a wall:
> Humpty Dumpty had a great fall.
> All the king's horses and all the king's men
> Couldn't put Humpty Dumpty in his place again. . . .'

'Don't stand chattering to yourself like that,' Humpty Dumpty said . . . 'but tell me your name and your business.'

'My *name* is Alice, but –'

'It's a stupid name enough!' Humpty Dumpty interrupted impatiently. 'What does it mean?'

'*Must* a name mean something?' Alice asked doubtfully.

'Of course it must,' Humpty Dumpty said with a short laugh, '*my* name means the shape I am – and a good handsome shape it is, too. With a name like yours, you might be any shape, almost.'

from Lewis Carroll, *Through the Looking Glass*

8   'Nadine, my dear, I am so glad to see you,' said Grandmother. Her voice had deepened with old age but lost none of its eager warmth, and it had gained that lilt of music that comes into the voices of the old when they are without querulousness. 'You're alone, dear?' 'Yes, Grandmother', replied Nadine. 'Did you expect me not to be?' 'I just thought, dear, that perhaps George and the children might have come

with you . . .' said Grandmother, trying to keep the disappointment out of her voice.

'The whole family would have been too much to inflict on you,' said Nadine lightly. 'And George can't leave the War Office. . . . Darling, how are you?'

And Nadine bent to kiss her mother-in-law with mingled love, resentment and exasperation. She did not deeply love Lucilla, but she did not forget that in the past, when it had come to a battle of wills between them, Grandmother had won, and she could never accept with acquiescence, as did the rest of the family, the fact that this frail old woman, sitting here in this absurd old-fashioned room, and never even raising her voice, moulded the entire Eliot clan as wax in her fingers.

from Elizabeth Goudge, *The Herb of Grace*

9   Lord,
        I feel such a fool
        talking to you,
        trying to believe.
        I'm not sure
        if you're listening
        or laughing
        or sleeping,
        or if you're there at all!

        I may as well be
        screaming at the wind.
        My words just blow away,
        drift away
        and die.

        But the silly thing about it is
        that I keep thinking about you!
        You slip through my doubts
        like a chink of light,
        like a haunting secret!

        If only I could be positive
        and really believe!
        I don't have faith like that,
        something solid and certain!

All I have is a funny feeling.
It's the kind of feeling you have
when you think you've met a certain
person before, but you can't quite visualize
the face or the time
or the place.
Yet somehow you know
this person knows you well.
And you could scream
because you can't quite open the door
and meet that person face to face.

Norman Habel, 'I feel such a fool trying to believe'

Meeting God in other people

In this passage, Michel Quoist, a French Catholic priest, urges Christians to be open to making contact with other people in a real way. If you are open to others, he says, you will find that you do not only meet the other person: you also meet God. The prayers and parable which follow say the same thing in a rather different way.

10   You will . . . have to welcome the other into your life. . . .
    You have to see to it that there is always room in your inn, that the door is always open. Let there be no need for a 'Beware of the Dog' sign in front of your home, whether that dog be your temperament, your pride, your egoism, your jealousy, your sarcasm, your gruffness, your tactlessness. . . . Don't hold back so that the other becomes hesitant; welcome him immediately into your life, if only by means of a handshake or a smile. . . .

    Start out on your day at peace, expectant, ready to receive the other in your life. Someone rings your bell, someone is knocking at your door. Please pass me the hammer. Mrs Jones, are you at home? Mr Smith, may I have a word with you, please? A book, the newspaper, the radio, a film, a billboard, or a smile – a moment of silence, a cutting word, a lowered head. It is the Lord – these are invitations to make contact.

from Michel Quoist, *The Christian Response*

11   I shook hands with my friend, Lord,
         And suddenly when I saw his sad and anxious face, I
            feared that you were not in his heart.
         I am troubled as I am before a closed tabernacle when
            there is no light to show that you are there.
         If you were not there, Lord, my friend and I would be
            separated.
         For his hand in mine would be only flesh in flesh
         And his love for me that of man for man.
         I want your life for him as well as for me.
         For it is only in you that he can be my brother.

         Michel Quoist, 'My Friend'

12   Here in the quietness, Lord, we are part of each other.
         Closer than lovers and loving close.
         Thanks, Lord, for being part of me, not just now,
         But in all the hurly-burly of life,
         For being present in the children's smile,
         The old man's whine, the mother's care.
         For being where men are, Lord,
         But most of all,
         For once
         Being man.

         Roger Bush, 'The Darkened Church'

13   Then the king will say to those on his right hand, 'You
         have my Father's blessing; come, enter and possess the
kingdom that has been ready for you since the world was made.
For when I was hungry, you gave me food; when thirsty, you
gave me drink; when I was a stranger you took me into your
home, when naked you clothed me; when I was ill you came to
my help, when in prison you visited me.' Then the righteous will
reply, 'Lord, when was it that we saw you hungry and fed you, or
thirsty and gave you drink, a stranger and took you home, or
naked and clothed you? When did we see you ill or in prison, and
come to visit you?' And the king will answer, 'I tell you this:
anything you did for one of my brothers here, however humble,
you did for me.'

Matthew 25: 34–40

Meeting the risen Jesus I

This story, told only by Luke, tells of the risen Jesus meeting his disciples on the way to Emmaus. It is when Jesus takes the bread, blesses, breaks and shares it in his characteristic way that the disciples realise who he is. Only at this point do they meet him in a real way.

14   That very same day, two of them were on their way to a village called Emmaus, seven miles from Jerusalem, and they were talking together about all that had happened. Now as they talked this over, Jesus himself came up and walked by their side; but something prevented them from recognising him. He said to them, 'What matters are you discussing as you walk along?' They stopped short, their faces downcast.

Then one of them, called Cleopas, answered him, 'You must be the only person staying in Jerusalem who does not know the things that have been happening there these last few days.' 'What things?' he asked. 'All about Jesus of Nazareth' they answered 'who proved he was a great prophet by the things he said and did in the sight of God and of the whole people; and how our chief priests and our leaders handed him over to be sentenced to death, and had him crucified. Our own hope had been that he would be the one to set Israel free. And this is not all: two whole days have gone by since it all happened; and some women from our group have astounded us: they went to the tomb in the early morning, and when they did not find the body, they came back to tell us they had seen a vision of angels who declared he was alive. Some of our friends went to the tomb and found everything exactly as the women had reported, but of him they saw nothing.'

Then he said to them, 'You foolish men! So slow to believe the full message of the prophets! Was it not ordained that the Christ should suffer and so enter into his glory?' Then, starting with Moses and going through all the prophets, he explained to them the passages throughout the scriptures that were about himself.

When they drew near to the village to which they were going, he made as if to go on; but they pressed him to stay with them. 'It is nearly evening' they said 'and the day is almost over.' So he went in to stay with them. Now while he was with them at table, he took the bread and said the blessing; then he broke it and handed it to them. And their eyes were opened and they recognised him; but he had vanished from their sight. Then they said to each other, 'Did not our hearts burn within us as he talked to us on the road and explained the scriptures to us?'

They set out that instant and returned to Jerusalem. There they found the Eleven assembled together with their companions, who said to them, 'Yes, it is true. The Lord has risen and has appeared to Simon.' Then they told their story of what had happened on the road and how they had recognised him at the breaking of the bread.

Luke 24: 13–35

Stuart Jackman's novel, *The Davidson Affair*, retells the story of Jesus' death and resurrection through the eyes of a TV camera lens. Cass Tennel interviews some of the key characters involved in the story. Among these is Cleopas, whom Luke tells us about in the Emmaus story. Here Cleopas gives his own account of meeting with Jesus in a somewhat different manner, surrounded by studio lights and camera crew:

15   'We were on the four o'clock bus to Emmaus, my brother-in-law and I. We'd been in town for the Festival, you see. We'd planned to go back home yesterday morning, but we hung on in case there was any more news.'

He was just as Kapper had described him on the phone, excited, transparently honest, bursting to tell his story. . . . Looking at him you felt that it was entirely appropriate – indeed almost inevitable – that he should have met God on a bus.

'News about the resurrection, you mean?' I said.

He nodded. 'That's right. We'd heard the rumour, of course. And naturally we were upset and confused. I was all for staying over until today, but my sister's a bit of a worrier and my brother-in-law thought it best that we should go home and perhaps come back in again this morning. . . .

'The bus was three parts empty,' he said, 'and we settled ourselves on the back seat and began to go over the events of the week-end again for about the ninety-ninth time. Trying to make some sort of sense out of it all, but not getting very far, I'm afraid.' He smiled apologetically. 'And then, about a mile out of the city, this man got on and came right down to the back and joined us.'

'Davidson?'

'Well, that's the funny thing. You see, we didn't recognise

him. We'd been followers of his for nearly two years. Not
important ones, don't run away with that idea. We're not in the
same class as Peter Johnson or Matthew Levison. But we
believed in him. We'd heard him speak dozens of times – never
missed the chance whenever he was anywhere near Jerusalem.
And we'd both talked to him personally on a number of occasions. But when he got on that bus yesterday afternoon he was
a complete stranger to us.' He shook his head impatiently, like a
man bewildered by his own stupidity. 'And there was something
else odd about it too. He didn't seem to have any idea at all about
what had been going on over the weekend in the city. He joined
in our conversation, but we had to tell him about the execution
last Friday and the rumours of yesterday's resurrection. From
the questions he asked he hadn't heard about any of it.'

'When you told him, what did he say?'

'Oh my word, Mr Tennel, what didn't he say? He started right
back there in the time of Moses and worked up through the
prophets – Isaiah and Amos – all the classic quotations – right
up to the present day. Had it all at his finger-tips. Marvellous. . . . All those bits and pieces of prophecy – the difficult
passages the priests spend half their lives discussing – he just
fitted them together like – well, like assembling one of those
do-it-yourself kits. Made the whole thing suddenly clear and
sort of – well, inevitable. Especially the resurrection.'. . .

I said slowly, 'I'd like to be quite clear about this, Mr Cleopas.
Are you saying that a resurrection is an integral part of the
Messiah story?'

'It's the climax of it. The final miraculous piece that makes
sense of all the rest.' He moved his hands in a gesture of rounded
completion. 'The Messiah comes, but nobody recognizes him.
Nobody wants him. He isn't in the least like we'd expected him
to be. Instead of crowning him king, we execute him. We don't
know who he is, so we get rid of him. Or try to. But Messiah is the
conqueror of death. And on the third day he comes back to
establish his kingdom.'

'Messiah is the conqueror of death'. They were the exact words
that Nicodemus had used. But for him they had been final proof
that Davidson was not – could not have been – the Messiah.
'Messiah cannot die' – that was what he had said. And if there
was no death in the Messiah story, how could there be a
resurrection?

I said, 'But if the Messiah is the conqueror of death, how can he die?'

'Unless he meets death face to face,' Simon Cleopas said, 'how can he conquer it?' . . .

He spoke the words with simple dignity, as relaxed and at home in front of the camera now as a news-reader. I had the odd feeling that our roles had been reversed; that he was somehow interviewing me. I shot a quick glance at the clock and said, 'And while he was explaining all of this, you still didn't recognize him?'

He nodded. 'Not until we got to Emmaus. He said he was going on up to Nazareth but my brother-in-law persuaded him to come home with us. "It'll only be pot-luck" he said, "but you're very welcome to share it." So he went with us to the house. And that's where it happened.'

'What exactly did happen there, Mr Cleopas?'

'We recognized him. At supper. We were sitting round the table ready to begin. My brother-in-law invited him, as the guest, to say grace. It's a custom we have among ourselves, you know. Well, he picked up the loaf, gave thanks, and broke it. And in that moment we looked at him and knew who he was.'

'Jesus Davidson?'

'Yes, of course, Jesus the Messiah. He was dead and is alive again. Blessed is he.'

from Stuart Jackman, *The Davidson Affair* (abridged)

Meeting the risen Jesus II

From the earliest days of the Church until today, people have been convinced of the reality of the risen Jesus by meeting with him.

16   Saul was still breathing murderous threats against the disciples of the Lord. He went to the High Priest and applied for letters to the synagogues at Damascus authorizing him to arrest anyone he found, men or women, who followed the new way, and bring them to Jerusalem. While he was still on the road and nearing Damascus, suddenly a light flashed from the sky all around him. He fell to the ground and heard a voice

saying, 'Saul, Saul, why do you persecute me?' 'Tell me, Lord,' he said, 'who you are.' The voice answered, 'I am Jesus, whom you are persecuting. But get up and go into the city, and you will be told what you have to do.' Meanwhile the men who were travelling with him stood speechless; they heard the voice but could see no one. Saul got up from the ground, but when he opened his eyes he could not see; so they led him by the hand and brought him into Damascus.

Acts 9: 1–8

17　　Let's put the question bluntly. . . . Is Christ really alive
　　　to-day, in this twentieth century?
　　　I don't mean can we treasure His words,
　　　　or try to follow His example,
　　　　　or imagine Him?
　　　I mean can we actually meet Him,
　　　　commune with Him,
　　　　　ask His help for our everyday affairs?

　　　The Gospel writers say 'yes'.
　　　A host of men and women down the ages say 'yes'.
　　　The Church says 'yes'.

The Church, you see, rests its unshakable conviction that fellowship of that kind with a living Lord is possible squarely on the fact of the Resurrection.

Now you may say that you believe in the Resurrection. But 'belief', as the New Testament writers use that word, implies more than intellectual assent.

It is a belief which becomes a deep inner knowing – a certainty...
　　a belief which reaches past the mind to the heart . . .
　　　a belief which flows directly into action.

from Peter Marshall, *Mr Jones, Meet the Master*

18　　Christ comes.
　　　Again and again he comes
　　　walking into our today
　　　challenging us, leading us, loving us
　　　into responding anew to his call. . . .

Hung on a cross
not to stay,
to return again each time we come
to lay our burdens there
and discover the way
to pick them up again
to go with lightness
forward, reborn. . . .

The Easter Christ:
dead and risen,
inviting us to leap
across the barriers into the tomorrow
of the Church:
with doors flung open
a place of sharing all
with all.

He comes
that we might live
to dream with daring,
and pray with hope
for a potency that creates
into reality a decent life
for all men.

Christ
    man
        comes . . .

Karol, 'He Comes'

19   We are once again pilgrims on the road to Emmaus. Our
      heads that were bowed, roused as we meet the Stranger
who draws near and comes with us. As evening comes, we strain
to make out his face while he talks to us, to our hearts; in
interpreting the Book of Life, he takes our broken hopes and
kindles them into fire: the way becomes lighter as, drawing the
embers together, we learn to fan the flame. If we invite him this
evening, he will sit down and together we shall share the meal.
And then all those who no longer believed will see and the hour
of Recognition will come. He will break the bread of tears at the

table of the poor and each will receive manna to his fill. We shall
return to Jerusalem to proclaim aloud what he has whispered in
our ear. And no doubt we shall find brothers there who will
reply: 'We too have met him.' For we know: the mercy of God has
come to visit the land of the living!

Isabelle, 'Meditation for our Journey'

When Christians meet together

The Acts of the Apostles tells how the early Christians met together to
share worship and the breaking of bread (no. 20). Then a French Catholic
priest compares the kind of meeting which takes place in two different
churches today (no. 21).

20   They met constantly to hear the apostles teach, and to
        share the common life, to break bread, and to pray. A
sense of awe was everywhere, and many marvels and signs were
brought about through the apostles. All whose faith had drawn
them together held everything in common: they would sell their
property and possessions and make a general distribution as the
need of each required. With one mind they kept up their daily
attendance at the temple, and, breaking bread in private
houses, shared their meals with unaffected joy, as they praised
God and enjoyed the favour of the whole people. And day by day
the Lord added to their number those whom he was saving.

Acts 2: 42–47

21   One Sunday I go to eleven o'clock mass in a neo-gothic
        city church. There are several hundred people there.
The first thing I see is their backs. The central nave looks as if it
is full. I don't want to sit in the side seats because I want to see. I
find a place at the back of the nave. I still see people's backs. At
the other end of the church I see the disused main altar. In front
of it I can just about see the ministers facing the people, but they
are very far away. What are they doing? I hear singing. A voice
comes over the loudspeakers. It must be the person's I see
standing at the microphone. Are the people singing in front of
me? Probably. I can't hear. At any rate the people round me are
silent. I'd like to sing but I'd feel I was singing solo and making a

fool of myself. Now come the readings and the sermon. I hear
them through the loudspeakers. But I feel distracted. I make an
effort to listen to the sermon. What is being said sounds intelli-
gent but this anonymous voice does not move me. What am I
doing there? If I'd stayed at home and watched it on television I
would probably have gained more from the sermon. . . .

On the following Sunday I try another church, in a neighbour-
ing district, which I have heard well spoken of. I enter the large
square hall with a wooden ceiling. Daylight enters through
invisible windows. The floor is sloped and the seats set in a
semi-circle. There are about a hundred people. I find a free seat.
The woman next to me smiles to show I can sit next to her. I
smile at her and sit down. The man on my left says good morning
and I return his greeting. I look up. I can see the whole assembly
at a glance. Young families, children, older people. They are
singing. The leader stands below in the middle of a semi-circle, a
few yards away from me. He sings: 'O Lord I come to you. . . .'
'And now all together.' Without realising it I find I am singing
with everyone else. I have joined in. We also sing the verses. My
neighbour shows me the book and the page. When the singing
stops, someone says: 'Good morning, brothers, may God's peace
and joy be with you!' The celebrant stretches out his arms to us
and smiles. He looks friendly. . . .

When I leave the church I feel I'd like to meet these people.
They are very willing. Everybody chats in the doorway. There is
a sort of courtyard with a coffee machine. Some are still discussing the gospel and what a young mother said about it. I think
I'll come back here another Sunday.

from Joseph Gelineau, *The Liturgy Today and Tomorrow* (abridged)

2
THE SYMBOL OF WATER

Look at your life. Look at the world in which you live your life: a world through which water flows – the immense oceans, the rivers that penetrate the land, the rain that nourishes the earth, the mists, clouds and dews that clothe the world.

Look at your life. See how you depend daily on water: to drink, to wash, to cool, to refresh, to nourish and to sustain life itself. See how water speaks to you deeply: as a symbol of purity, of refreshment, of cleansing, of new life.

Look at your life, says the Christian, and begin to feel the power of the mighty flood in the beginning, the mysterious waters of baptism, and the living water which Jesus brings.

Water: a simple necessity

The world depends upon water for life. In the following passage Debbie Taylor shows how vital water is for survival and how many people are denied their right to one of the simplest necessities of life (no. 22). Then a telephone engineer from Croydon and a farmer from Botswana speak of what water means to their lives (no. 23).

22   A sheet of water is like a pane of glass – smooth, colourless, flawless. Dip your hand into it, bring it to your lips – no smell, no taste. And, almost before you have sipped, it has slipped through your fingers back into the lake.

Almost the simplest substance on earth – just two molecules of hydrogen and one of oxygen – combine to make something hard and cold as ice, burning and ephemeral as steam, a sparkle of tiny droplets from the splash in a swimming pool. Or a hole of stinking black mud, a dank green pool at the bottom of a well, the yellow-brown seepage from a hollow scratched in the dry river bed.

Water drops from the skies, flows freely in rivers, bursts from the ground in springs. And there is more than enough for everyone. Surely something so simple, so abundant and free cannot be perverted? Yet in many countries water is used – not just for quenching thirst and washing clothes – but as a weapon that serves the powerful at the expense of the weak.

Driven from the rivers of their lush home-lands, Bushmen and Aborigines now roam the burning deserts of Africa and Australia in search of water, or beg it from wells drilled for the new rulers of their land.

Water, so vital for life, becomes an instrument of power as soon as it is concentrated in a form that can be controlled. Free while still in the clouds, there is a price when it flows from the dam into irrigation canals. Free while it slowly percolates down through layers of soil, there is a price when it is coaxed to the surface again by well or pump.

Without air we die in three minutes; without water we die in three days. Without *clean* water death can come after fifty years of suffering with bilharzia or guinea worm – or at the age of six months after a short, sharp dose of diarrhoea. The World Health Organisation estimates that over three-quarters of all diseases are caused by dirty drinking water, insufficient water for washing and inadequate sanitation. So water is not only vital for life, but vital for health too. It is just too important to be left to the market place.

from Debbie Taylor, 'Pure and simple'

23   Harry Watkins, Telephone engineer, Croydon, UK; 'What? What do you mean where does it come from? Reservoirs, I suppose. I think they catch the rain, purify it, then send it through pipes. Hot water's expensive I can tell you. You should see my electricity bill! Cold water? I don't know. I suppose they include it in the rates. Of course there's enough – except for the drought in 1976. That was terrible. They stopped people washing their cars and watering their gardens. We'd booked a canal holiday but had to cancel, the water was so low in the canals the boats kept getting stuck!'

Stephina Mapogo, Farmer, Molepolole, Botswana; 'Look at this earth. It is hard and dry. People call this part of Botswana the "great thirstland" because there are no rivers here. Last month there was no rain to make the ground soft for planting. Now you can see my plants are small and green. But without rain they will die – only rich people can afford to have a borehole drilled for their crops. Now look at the sky – how clear and blue it is. Where is the rain to save my seedlings? When it rains we run out to feel the rain on our faces – no-one minds getting wet when it rains. We call the rain "pula". Our money we call pula too. Water and money. It's all the same to us. Without rain there is no food, no work, no money.'

from 'People, Water and Ways of Life'

Images of water I

Water is not only a basic requirement for existence. It is also a powerful natural element which has always compelled human fascination and wonder through its great variety and beauty. Rain, river, springs and sea suggest a variety of images to the writers of the following extracts.

24   I sit by a little stream and I look at the water. It keeps on flowing past me. It comes from a spring that is invisible to me. But it must rise somewhere.

    I look into the water. The water is clear, pure. . . . There are stones lying in the water, scoured smooth and polished by it. I can see the bed of the stream: how deep can the stream be? On its surface it carries all sorts of things along with it, leaves, bits of twig, little plants, roots and all. Before long many of these little streams will meet and grow into a river that empties itself into the sea. And then the water will carry ships and people on its back and bear them across the world.

I take some of the water into my hands. It is fresh, cool and clear. I feel the water flowing through my fingers. It carries away the dust on my hands. I bring the water to my face, as I do each day. The water cleanses me as nothing else can. . . . I cup my hands and drink the water from them. It tastes good. It quenches my thirst. . . . I smell the water. It has no scent at all. Or has it? Yes, it has a scent, a quite extraordinary scent that is there and yet is not there. It smells of moss and herbs and grass. It is not possible to describe this scent in words. It is simply freshness itself or should I try to put it another way? The water smells of depth, of simplicity, of distance. . . .

I listen to the stream. It laps against the banks. It is a beautiful sound, not a rushing sound, nor singing, nor murmuring. It is a babbling sound. Sounds that are for ever altering like the ripples on the water. And while I am occupying myself with the water I think of the poet who said, 'When the soul listens it is already speaking a living language.' And I experience the water as an image of myself.

from J. de Rooy, *Tools for Meditation*

25   The sea is a hungry dog,
        Giant and grey.
        He rolls on the beach all day.
        With his clashing teeth and shaggy jaws
        Hour upon hour he gnaws
        The rumbling, tumbling stones,
        And 'Bones, bones, bones, bones!'
        The giant sea-dog moans,
        Licking his greasy paws.

        And when the night wind roars
        And the moon rocks in the stormy cloud,

He bounds to his feet and snuffs and sniffs,
Shaking his wet sides over the cliffs,
And howls and hollos long and loud.

But on quiet days in May or June,
When even the grasses on the dune
Play no more their reedy tune,
With his head between his paws
He lies on the sandy shores,
So quiet, so quiet, he scarcely snores.

James Reeves, 'The Sea'

26   In an enclosure of rocks the peaks of the water romped
and wandered and a light crown of tufty scum standing
high on the surface kept slowly turning round: chips of it blew
off and gadded about without weight in the air . . . the crests I
saw ravelled up by the wind into the air in arching whips and
straps of glassy spray and higher broken into clouds of white and
blown away. Under the curl shone a bright juice of beautiful
green.

from *Gerard Manley Hopkins: Poems and Prose*

27   After the beautiful rain,
The rocks shine under the sun,
Like the droplets on the cobweb
Amongst the green, green grass.

Geeta Mohanty, aged 13, 'Pearls on the grass'

28   Between
        slats of the garden
        bench, and strung
        to their undersides
        ride clinging
        rain-drops, white
        with transmitted
        light as the bench
        with paint: ranged
        irregularly
        seven staves of them
        shine out
        against the space
        behind: untroubled
        by the least breeze they
        seem not to move
        but one
        by one as if
        suddenly ripening
        tug themselves free
        and splash
        down to be
        replaced by an identical
        and instant twin:
        the longer you
        look at it
        the stillness proves
        one flow unbroken
        of new, false pearls,
        dropped seeds of now
        becoming then.

        Charles Tomlinson 'During Rain'

29   Whirl up, sea —
        Whirl your pointed pines
        Splash your great pines
        On our rocks,
        Hurl your green over us,
        Cover us with your pools of fir.

        H.D., 'Oread'

30   Are you alive?
        I touch you.
        You quiver like a sea-fish.
        I cover you with my net.
        What are you – banded one?

H.D., 'The Pool'

Images of water II

Water provides powerful images not only for the poet, but also for the religious believer. The following extracts make use of the image of water to suggest different aspects of the believer's relationship with God and other people.

31   Lord, thou art like a mighty River, All-knowing,
            All-seeing,
        And I like a tiny fish in thy vast waters,
        How shall I gauge thy depths?
        How shall I reach thy shores?
        Wherever I go, I see thee only,
        And when snatched out of thy waters I die of
            separation.

A Sikh hymn

32   Protect me, O Lord;
        My boat is so small,
        And your sea is so big.

The Fisherman's Prayer

33   As a doe longs
            for running streams,
        so longs my soul
            for you, my God.

        My soul thirsts for God,
            the God of life.

Psalm 42: 1–2

34   Are you fond of the sea?

Think of a glorious stretch of coast-line somewhere and settle down before it as if you were going to paint a picture of it. Choose a sunny, tranquil day on which to see it, so that everything will be clear for you.

Notice how beautifully the land and water masses are arranged, and how quietly the sky rests on both. . . . Think of the colour and light everywhere, the unusual scents and sounds, the freedom and the freshness and the wonderful sense of swing and flow and life everywhere. . . .

Turn your attention now to any little inshore wave on the beach, lake-side or pond-edge: notice that the water looks too lazy to rise up, but it does, and we see a line of light along its crest; it creams over and swishes back through the sand.

A rising and falling and a little pause for recharge – that is the wave shape. We find this in that little inshore wave, but also in the great rollers and combers out at sea. . . .

Our breathing too is a wave form and as we lie there, life flows gently in and then out again, with a short pause before flowing in once more. . . .

Since with every breath I draw, this real miracle of New Life . . . comes flowing into me and through me, I receive it thankfully, and offer it up again, freely, quietly as it came to me. And the moment's pause before once more I receive it, begins to be an act of Trust in the Giver of Life, the Father of everyone of us, in whom we all quite truly live, move and have our being – as if we were in an inexhaustible ocean of Life and Light, Love, Strength and Joy which is our home.

from Sonia Syner, *Relaxation*

35   Lord, I saw the sea attacking the rocks, sombre and
            raging.
         From afar the waves gained momentum.
         High and proud, they leapt, jostling one another to be
            the first to strike.
         When the white foam drew back, leaving the rock
            clear, they gathered themselves to rush forward
            again.

The other day I saw the sea, calm and serene.
The waves came from afar, creeping, not to draw
attention.
Quietly holding hands, they slipped noiselessly and
stretched at full length on the sand, to touch the
shore with the tips of their beautiful, soft fingers.
The sun gently caressed them, and they generously
returned streams of light.

Lord, grant that I may avoid useless quarrels that tire
and wound without achieving results.
Keep me from these angry outbursts that draw
attention but leave one uselessly weakened.
Keep me from wanting always to outstrip others in my
conceit, crushing those in my way.
Wipe from my face the look of dark, dominating anger.
Rather, Lord, grant that I may live my days calmly and
fully, as the sea slowly covers the whole shore.
Make me humble like the sea, as, silently and gently,
it spreads out, unnoticed.
May I wait for my brothers and match my pace to
theirs, that I may move upward with them.
Grant me the triumphant perseverance of the waters.
May each of my retreats turn into an advance.
Give my face the light of clear waters.
Give my soul the whiteness of foam.
Illumine my life that it may sing like sunbeams on the
surface of the sea.
But above all, Lord, may I not keep this light for
myself, and may all those who come near me return
home eager to bathe in your eternal grace.

Michel Quoist, 'The Sea'

Waters of destruction

Many ancient religious traditions speak of a great flood at the beginning of time when the gods destroyed the world. These ancient myths emphasise the destructive powers of water, and the judgement of God. But the flood is not the end of the story: out of the destruction a new world and a new beginning emerge. Here are extracts from two flood stories: one from the Bible (no. 36), and one from the Epic of Gilgamesh (no. 37). Then Rex Chapman meditates on the meaning of the flood (no. 38).

36   Towards the end of seven days the waters of the flood came upon the earth. . . . All the springs of the great abyss broke through, the windows of the sky were opened, and rain fell on the earth for forty days and forty nights. On that very day Noah entered the ark with his sons Shem, Ham and Japheth, his own wife, and his three sons' wives. Wild animals of every kind, cattle of every kind, reptiles of every kind that move upon the ground, and birds of every kind – all came to Noah in the ark. . . . The flood continued upon the earth for forty days, and the waters swelled and lifted up the ark so that it rose high above the ground. They swelled and increased over the earth, and the ark floated on the surface of the waters. More and more the waters increased until they covered all the high mountains everywhere under heaven. . . . Every living creature that moves on earth perished, birds, cattle, wild animals, all reptiles, and all mankind. Everything died that had the breath of life in its nostrils, everything on dry land. God wiped out every living thing that existed on earth . . . and only Noah and his company in the ark survived.

When the waters had increased over the earth for a hundred and fifty days, God thought of Noah and all the wild animals and cattle with him in the ark, and he made a wind pass over the earth and the waters began to subside. The springs of the abyss were stopped up, and so were the windows of the sky; the downpour from the skies was checked. The water gradually receded from the earth, and by the end of a hundred and fifty days it had disappeared. On the seventeenth day of the seventh month the ark grounded on a mountain in Ararat.

Genesis 7:10–8:4 (abridged)

37   With the first light of dawn a black cloud came from the
       horizon; it thundered within where Adad, lord of the
storm was riding. In front over hill and plain Shullat and
Hanish, heralds of the storm, led on. Then the gods of the abyss
rose up; Nergal pulled out the dams of the nether waters,
Ninurta the war-lord threw down the dykes, and the seven
judges of hell, the Annunaki, raised their torches, lighting the
land with their vivid flame. A stupor of despair went up to
heaven when the god of the storm turned daylight to darkness,
when he smashed the land like a cup. One whole day the tempest
raged gathering fury as it went, it poured over the people like
the tides of battle; a man could not see his brother nor the people
be seen from heaven. Even the gods were terrified at the
flood. . . .

For six days and six nights the winds blew, torrent and
tempest and flood overwhelmed the world, tempest and flood
raged together like warring hosts. When the seventh day
dawned the storm from the south subsided, the sea grew calm,
the flood was stilled; I looked at the face of the world and there
was silence, all mankind was turned to clay.

from *The Epic of Gilgamesh*

38   The forces of chaos shatter all order.
       They seek to drown a man's hopes, his plans, his career.
       They well up inside and out to destroy all in their path.
       They despoil the very necessities of life.
       They leave behind them a train of refugees fleeing
            from war.
       They bring a man's life to a halt in a crisis of\indecision.
       It is as if you were displeased with your creation, Lord,
            and were bringing it to nought.
       And yet for the man who is ready these same forces
            sweep him on his way to the re-creation of life.
       Chaos contains within it the slight glimmer of hope.
       Lord, you are there.
       You are in life.
       You are in the Flood.
       You are in the midst.
       Send me, send everyman, the dove with the olive leaf
            in its mouth.

Waters of salvation

Crossing water or passing through water is a powerful symbol for new beginnings, or in religious language for 'salvation'. In Richard Adams' novel *Watership Down* the river marks the new beginning for the dispossessed band of rabbits (no. 39). In the Old Testament, the Red Sea marks the new beginning for the Israelites (nos. 40, 41). In the New Testament the theme is continued when Jesus brings the disciples safely across the raging sea (no. 42).

39   Hazel came out on the farther side of the ilexes and followed the path round a bend. Then he stopped dead and sat back on his haunches. Immediately in front of him, Bigwig and Dandelion were staring out from the sheer edge of a high bank, and below the bank ran a stream. It was in fact the little river Enborne, twelve to fifteen feet wide and at this time of year two or three feet deep with spring rain, but to the rabbits it seemed immense, such a river as they had never imagined. . . .

'What do you think we ought to do now, Fiver?' asked Hazel.

Fiver looked down at the water and twitched his ears.

'We shall have to cross it,' he said. 'But I don't think I can swim, Hazel, I'm worn out, and Pipkin's a good deal worse than I am.'

'Cross it?' cried Bigwig. 'Cross it? Who's going to cross it? What do you want to cross it for? I never heard such nonsense.'

Like all wild animals, rabbits can swim if they have to. . . . But most rabbits avoid swimming. . . .

Hazel moved close to Fiver and quietly edged him away from the others. . . . 'Are you sure we've got to cross the river, Fiver? What about going along the bank one way or the other?'

'No, we need to cross the river, Hazel, so that we can get into those fields – and on beyond them too. I know what we ought to be looking for – a high, lonely place with dry soil, where rabbits can see and hear all round and men hardly ever come. Wouldn't that be worth a journey?'

from Richard Adams, *Watership Down*

40   In days when artificial boundaries and frontiers were hard to create, water was the most obvious and effective dividing-line known to man. . . . To pass from one territory to another it was necessary to go through the water. This passage

might be made by wading or by finding a shallow ford or by swimming or by constructing a boat. In whatever way it was made, it was a dramatic experience to pass from one region to another, especially if the territory to which the journey was made had never been explored before. No symbolism could more effectively portray a passage from the old to the new, from the well-known to the unknown, from the bounded to the free, as could a passage through the water. He who had crossed the water had separated himself from the old and was henceforth committed to the new.

Nowhere in the ancient world does this general pattern find more dramatic expression than in the experience of the Hebrew tribes. Imprinted on their memory was the succession of episodes which is recorded in the early chapters of the Book of Exodus . . . that a band of Hebrews was enslaved in Egypt, that under the leadership of Moses they made a bid for freedom and that their escape was dramatically sealed by a passage through the waters of the Red Sea which effectively separated them from their wretched past and opened the way to a future of promise and hope. . . . The fact that God had brought them through the waters was for ever afterwards connected with their beginnings as a distinctive people and with the heritage of free movement which they believed was their due. . . . Through the waters of Jordan they had crossed the boundary. Separated from their past they looked forward once again to their future with hope and expectancy.

from F. W. Dillistone, *Christianity and Symbolism*

41 O give thanks to the Lord, for he is good:
    for his mercy endures for ever.

    Who struck down Egypt and its firstborn:
    for his mercy endures for ever;

    Who brought out Israel from among them:
    for his mercy endures for ever,

    With strong hand and with outstretched arm:
    for his mercy endures for ever;

Who divided the Red Sea into two parts:
for his mercy endures for ever,

And made Israel pass through the midst of it:
for his mercy endures for ever;

Who remembered us in our humiliation:
for his mercy endures for ever,

And delivered us from our enemies:
for his mercy endures for ever.

Psalm 136 (abridged)

42   One day he got into a boat with his disciples, and he said
to them, 'Let us go across to the other side of the lake.' So
they set out, and as they sailed he fell asleep. And a storm of
wind came down on the lake, and they were filling with water,
and were in danger. And they went and woke him saying,
'Master, Master, we are perishing!' And he awoke and rebuked
the wind and the raging waves; and they ceased, and there was a
calm. He said to them, 'Where is your faith?' And they were
afraid, and they marvelled, saying to one another, 'Who then is
this, that he commands even wind and water, and they obey
him?'

Luke 8: 22–25

Waters of baptism

In the sacrament of baptism the Christian passes through water to make a
new beginning as a member of Christ's church. The first four passages
illustrate the practice of baptism in the New Testament and in the church
today (nos 43–46). Then the following extracts reflect on the meaning of
baptism (nos. 47–50).

43   The beginning of the Good News about Jesus Christ, the
Son of God. It is written in the book of the prophet
Isaiah: 'Look, I am going to send my messenger before you; he
will prepare your way. A voice cries in the wilderness: Prepare a
way for the Lord, make his paths straight', and so it was that

John the Baptist appeared in the wilderness, proclaiming a baptism of repentance for the forgiveness of sins. All Judaea and all the people of Jerusalem made their way to him, and as they were baptised by him in the river Jordan they confessed their sins. John wore a garment of camel-skin, and he lived on locusts and wild honey. In the course of his preaching he said, 'Someone is following me, someone who is more powerful than I am, and I am not fit to kneel down and undo the strap of his sandals. I have baptised you with water, but he will baptise you with the Holy Spirit.'

It was at this time that Jesus came from Nazareth in Galilee and was baptised in the Jordan by John. No sooner had he come up out of the water than he saw the heavens torn apart and the Spirit, like a dove, descending on him. And a voice came from heaven, 'You are my Son, the Beloved; my favour rests on you.' Immediately afterwards the Spirit drove him out into the wilderness and he remained there for forty days, and was tempted by Satan. He was with the wild beasts, and the angels looked after him.

Mark 1: 1–13

44   Philip began to speak; starting from this passage of scripture, he told the official the Good News about Jesus. As they travelled down the road, they came to a place where there was some water, and the official said, 'Here is some water. What is to keep me from being baptized?'

The official ordered the carriage to stop, and both Philip and the official went down into the water, and Philip baptized him. When they came up out of the water, the Spirit of the Lord took Philip away. The official did not see him again, but continued on his way, full of joy.

Acts 8: 35–39

45   I was baptized into the Strict Baptists . . . in 1950. . . . If you want to become a member of our church, first of all you must tell the pastor and he will tell you that you must be baptized by total immersion in our pool. You've got to have courage to face this. But before this happens, the pastor tells the full church that you want to join it and the church then says that two 'Messengers' are to be sent to you. . . . They see you in your

home and hear why you want to join the church and listen to you make your confession of Christ as Saviour. . . . Then you come into the church and take up a position in front of all the members and give an account of yourself. A lot of folk can't face this. . . . Well, after you have come before the church and have been accepted, the pastor says, 'When would you like to be baptized?'

The baptism usually takes place a fortnight later at the close of the Sunday evening service. You'll get people coming just out of curiosity and there'll be plenty of children present just because of the novelty. And you'll get the regular old diehard Baptists from all around. . . . So the church is packed. Well now, just imagine yourself. You've confided to the Messengers, you've stood in front of about forty village people and given your testimony, and now you've got to step out in front of everybody you know for miles around, and dressed in a white cricket outfit, and again be asked if you own the Lord. You say yes, so the pastor will say, 'Then do you want to be buried with the Lord?' Again you say yes. Then he says, 'Shall we go down on to the water together?' And you are taken under. . . . The Sunday following the baptism, the new member is given a set of the church rules and told that he must help run and pay for the church.

from 'The Baptist Deacon' in Ronald Blythe, *Akenfield: Portrait of an English Village*

46   'We christened our daughter Susan' one overhears a mother say in a queue at a bus-stop. What on earth has actually been happening to this baby who has been 'christened'?

One error is easily put right. Susan did not get her name at this 'christening' – she was given it by her parents soon after birth, and was registered as 'Susan', and would have been called 'Susan' even if she had never been 'christened'. So what was the 'christening'? Literally it was a 'Christ-ing' of her . . . the meaning of it is 'becoming Christ's'. . . .

Within the Christian family the baptism of infants is a sign that they will be brought up *as believers*, at one with their parents in their faith in the living God. And this is in fact how believers do bring up their children – to call God their 'Father' right from the start. There is no point where consciousness begins, or faith 'starts' – so the only point for initiation by baptism is immediately after birth.

from Colin Buchanan, 'Initiation Services', in *Anglican Worship Today*

47   The priest stands before the water of baptism and says:

Almighty God, whose Son Jesus Christ was baptized in
the river Jordan;
we thank you for the gift of water to cleanse us and
revive us;
we thank you that through the waters of the Red Sea,
you led your people out of slavery to freedom in the
promised land;
we thank you that through the deep waters of death
you brought your Son, and raised him to life in
triumph.
Bless this water, that your servants who are washed in
it may be made one with Christ in his death and in
his resurrection, to be cleansed and delivered from
all sin.
Send your Holy Spirit upon them to bring them to new
birth in the family of your Church, and raise them
with Christ to full and eternal life.
For all might, majesty, authority, and power are yours,
now and for ever.   Amen.

from the Baptism Service, *The Alternative Service Book 1980*

48   Baptism is a dying to self and a being reborn to a new life
in Christ. The going down into the waters symbolizes a
burial and the coming up from the waters a resurrection. There
is thus a new creation; a new person is made.

from Alan Richardson, *A Dictionary of Christian Theology*

49   It represents death and burial, life and resurrection . . .
when we plunge our head into water as into a tomb, the
old man is immersed, wholly buried; when we come out of the
water, the new man appears at that moment.

John Chrysostom

50   I am free!

I was born free.
No, I didn't free myself.
I entered the waters of death

and I drowned.
I died with Christ,
and Christ died with me.
We went through hell together.

But His tomb is also a womb.
The waters of death
are also waters of life.
He was there.
He spoke to the waters of the deep
and life began,
when the world was first born
and I was freeborn.

I was born free.
I rose with Christ
like a spring from the deep,
like an infant from the womb,
like a new first man.
I rose a new me,
a new man,
a free king.

People keep telling me
that I'm not really free.
My old me keeps reminding me
of wrongs I do each day:
'You're fooling yourself.
You aren't really free.'

Oh, but I am!
We all are.
We were born free in baptism.

We rose free in Christ.
And He is free to free all men.
We are free!
No sin, law, old self,
or new fear,
can ever bind us forever.

Never! Never! Never!
We ARE born free.
WE ARE!

Norman Habel, 'Born Free: A Baptismal Shout'

Water as a powerful religious symbol

The following two extracts reflect on how and why it is that water appears
as such a powerful symbol in the great religions of the world.

51   A most important feature of symbols lies in their richness of expression. They have what Josiah Royce calls
'surplus meaning', the ability to speak to man of many things.
Whereas a sign must refer specifically to one object, person or
event, a symbol is able to refer to a variety of things at different
times and places. Whereas the sign has a one-to-one relationship, the symbol has a one-to-many relationship. In fact a true
symbol appears to be always capable of new applications and
evocative of new insights. Water confronts man in his existence
in many different ways. Sometimes water is cool and refreshing,
suggesting the beneficence of creation. In the midst of flood or
storms at sea, water assumes a malevolent aspect and symbolizes the ultimate threat to man's existence. It is hardly surpris-
ing that water should be a universal symbol and most ambiva-
lent in its meaning, at one time suggesting life and regenera-
tion, at another destruction and death. . . .

This ambivalence of symbols is partly due to differences in
geographical and cultural environments. The environment of
the Babylonians led them to stress the character of water as a
symbol of destruction, for they were constantly threatened by
the overthrow of their homes by flood. In Egypt and Palestine,
on the other hand, no such terror of water was normally experienced, and in these countries water usually symbolized the
creativity of nature. . . .

The significance of a symbol is not unlimited. It has both
flexibility and constancy. The 'multiplicity of signification' is
bounded by 'the natural qualities of the symbol'. A symbol
operates because it bears a relationship with that symbolized.

This lays a limit upon its use. The symbol can only reveal what is present within it.

from Thomas Fawcett, *The Symbolic Language of Religion*

52   Water symbolises the whole of potentiality ... the source of all possible existence.... Waters are the foundations of the whole world ... they ensure long life and creative energy, they are the principle of all healing.... In initiation rituals, water confers a 'new birth', in magic rituals it heals, and in funeral rites it assures rebirth after death.... Symbol of creation, harbour of all seeds, water becomes the supreme magic and medicinal substance; it heals, it restores youth, it ensures eternal life.

from Mircea Eliade, *Patterns in Comparative Religion*

The promise of 'living water'

In the Bible God promises 'living water' to his thirsty people. Christians believe that Jesus has fulfilled this promise.

53   The poor and needy ask for water, and there is none,
      their tongue is parched with thirst.
      I, Yahweh, will answer them,
      I, the God of Israel, will not abandon them.

      I will make rivers well up on barren heights,
      and fountains in the midst of valleys;
      turn the wilderness into a lake,
      and dry ground into waterspring.

      I will pour out water on the thirsty soil,
      streams on the dry ground.
      I will pour my spirit on your descendants,
      my blessing on your children.
      They shall grow like grass where there is
           plenty of water,
      like poplars by running streams.

      Those he led through the deserts never went
           thirsty;

he made water spring for them from the rock,
he split the rock and water flowed.

Jesus said, 'Whoever drinks this water
   will get thirsty again;
but anyone who drinks the water that I shall give
will never be thirsty again:
the water that I shall give
will turn into a spring inside him, welling
   up to eternal life.'

Isaiah 41: 17–18; 44: 3–4; 48: 21; John 4: 13–14

54   I heard the voice of Jesus say,
       'Behold, I freely give
       The living water, thirsty one,
       Stoop down and drink, and live'.
       I came to Jesus and I drank
       Of that life-giving stream;
       My thirst was quenched, my soul revived,
       And now I live in him.

Horatius Bonar

3
THE PRESENCE OF MYSTERY

Look at your life: see how it is full of mystery and awe. Everyday experiences and the hum-drum world around you are charged with a mysterious depth and presence.

Look at your life: see how it is full of mystery and awe. Unexpected happenings, puzzling occurrences, old things seen in a new way: mystery lies at the heart of your life. It beckons you closer, yet you draw back afraid. What is this experience of depth and presence?

Look at your life, says the Christian. See how, at the heart of the mystery, a personal presence greets you and demands your response. It is Christ himself, who reveals the greatest mystery of all: the mystery of God's love, the love which you cannot ignore, the love towards which you are irresistibly attracted and yet before which you tremble in fear.

Approaching the mystery

There are numerous objects and experiences to ponder over and to wonder about in our ordinary, everyday world. In the following four passages, different writers describe occasions when the ordinary world fascinated and puzzled them with a sense of mystery, and each describes a unique response to this mystery.

55   Why, who makes much of a miracle?
      As to me I know of nothing else but miracles,
      Whether I walk the streets of Manhattan,
      Or dart my sight over the roofs of houses toward the
          sky,
      Or wade with naked feet along the beach just in the
          edge of the water,
      Or stand under trees in the woods . . .
      Or watch honey-bees busy around the hive of a
          summer fore-noon,
      Or animals feeding in the fields,
      Or birds, or the wonderfulness of insects in the air,
      Or the wonderfulness of the sundown, or of stars
          shining so quiet and bright,
      Or the exquisite delicate thin curve of the new moon in
          spring. . . .

      To me every hour of the light and dark is a miracle,
      Every cubic inch of space is a miracle,
      Every square yard of the surface of the earth is spread
          with the same,
      Every foot of the interior swarms with the same.

      To me the sea is a continual miracle,
      The fishes that swim – the rocks – the motion of the
          waves – the ships with men in them,
      What stranger miracles are there?

      Walt Whitman, 'Miracles'

56   I took my mind a walk
      Or my mind took me a walk –
      Whichever was the truth of it.

The light glittered on the water
Or the water glittered in the light.
Cormorants stood on a tidal rock

With their wings spread out,
Stopping no traffic. Various ducks
Shilly-shallied here and there

On the shilly-shallying water.
An occasional gull yelped. Small flowers
Were doing their level best

To bring to their kerb bees like
Aerial charabancs. Long weeds in the clear
Water did Eastern dances, unregarded

By shoals of darning needles. A cow
Started a moo but thought
Better of it. . . . And my feet took me home

And my mind observed to me,
Or I to it, how ordinary
Extraordinary things are or

How extraordinary ordinary
Things are, like the nature of the mind
And the process of observing.

Norman MacCaig, 'An Ordinary Day'

57   The night was rising, like a dark smoke, and already
filling the valleys, which could no longer be dis-
tinguished from the plains. The villages were lighting up,
greeting each other across the dusk like constellations. With a
flick of his finger Fabien blinked his wing-lights in answer. The
earth was now dotted with luminous appeals, each house now
lighting up its star against the immensity of the night, much as
a beacon is trained upon the sea. Everything that sheltered
human life now sparkled; and Fabien was overjoyed that his
entry into the night should this time be slow and beautiful, like
an entry into port.

He ducked his head down inside the cockpit. The phosphor-
escent needles had begun to glow. One after the other he
checked the figures and was happy. He felt himself solidly
ensconced in this evening sky. He ran a finger along a steel rib

and felt the life coursing through it; the metal was not vibrant but alive. The engine's five hundred horse-power had charged the matter with a gentle current, changing its icy deadness into velvet flesh. Once again the pilot in flight experienced neither giddiness nor intoxicating thrill, but only the mysterious travail of living flesh.

He had made a world for himself once more. He moved his arms to feel even more at home, then ran his thumb over the electric circuit diagram. . . . Attentive to dial readings, he could now enter the night, like a submarine starting on its dive. There was no trembling, no shaking, no undue vibration; and as his gyroscope, altimeter, and r.p.m. rate remained constant, he stretched his limbs, leaned his head back against the leather seat, and fell into an airborne meditation rich with unfathomable hopes.

Now, swallowed up by the night like a watchman, he could see how the night betrays man's secrets: those appeals, those lights, that anxiety. That single star down there in the shadow – a house in isolation. That other star flickering and going out – a house closing the shutters on its love. Or on its boredom. A house that has ceased signalling to the rest of the world. Gathered around their lamp-lit table, those farmers little guessed the true measure of their hopes nor realized how far their yearnings reached in the great night that encompassed them. But Fabien, approaching from six hundred miles away, uncovered them along with the ground-swells that lifted and lowered his breathing plane. Having traversed ten storms, like battlefields, and the moonlit clearings between them, he now picked up these lights, one after another, with a pride of conquest. Down there they thought their lamp was lit for their humble table, but already from fifty miles away one was touched by its desolate appeal, as though they were desperately swinging it, from a deserted island, at the dark immensity of the sea.

from Antoine de Saint-Exupéry, *Night Flight*

58   One summer evening . . . I found
         A little boat tied to a willow tree
         Within a rocky cave, its usual home.
         Straight I unloosed her chain, and stepping in
         Pushed from the shore. It was an act of stealth

And troubled pleasure, nor without the voice
Of mountain-echoes did my boat move on;
Leaving behind her still, on either side,
Small circles glittering idly in the moon,
Until they melted all into one track
Of sparkling light. But now, like one who rows,
Proud of his skill, to reach a chosen view
Upon the summit of a craggy ridge,
The horizon's utmost boundary; far above
Was nothing but the stars and the grey sky.
She was an elfin pinnace; lustily
I dipped my oars into the silent lake,
And, as I rose upon the stroke, my boat
Went heaving through the water like a swan;
When, from behind that craggy steep till then
The horizon's bound, a huge peak, black and huge,
As if with voluntary power instinct,
Upreared its head. I struck and struck again,
And growing still in stature the grim shape
Towered up between me and the stars, and still,
For so it seemed, with purpose of its own
And measured motion like a living thing,
Strode after me. With trembling oars I turned,
And through the silent water stole my way
Back to the covert of the willow tree;
There in her mooring-place I left my bark, –
And through the meadows homeward went, in grave
And serious mood; but after I had seen
That spectacle, for many days, my brain
Worked with a dim and undetermined sense
Of unknown modes of being; o'er my thoughts
There hung a darkness, call it solitude
Or blank desertion. No familiar shapes
Remained, no pleasant images of trees,
Of sea or sky, no colours of green fields;
But huge and mighty forms, that do not live
Like living men, moved slowly through the mind
By day, and were a trouble to my dreams.

from William Wordsworth, 'The Prelude'

Encountering the presence at the heart of the mystery

The following passages probe more deeply the meaning behind the mystery in our world. They describe a sense of purpose behind the mystery, a sense of presence within the mystery. This is glimpsed obscurely at first, until in David Porter's poem (no. 62) a living, personal presence is revealed at the heart of the mystery.

59   Three individuals describe their experiences of mystery:

. . . I woke up once when I was nine or ten in the middle of the night and wrote a poem out of the blue; and the fact that I did that has always seemed very odd to me, because the poem sort of came 'whole'. I suppose you could call it a sort of mystical poem because it didn't have anything that I could relate it to; it was a kind of mystical vision of space.

. . . I was alone, and I was walking down the village. I felt perfectly at home; I've always loved the dark; I've always loved silence. And there were these beautiful colours, which gave me a feeling of reverence for the whole of creation. And then I asked other people, 'Wasn't the sky beautiful tonight?' And they said, 'What sky?' It baffled me no end, but even so it was years before I realised that I had really seen something which other people presumably had not, and which in fact had not physically existed.

. . . there are times when I just feel the presence, if that's the word; it just happens. It's marvellous. It's terribly clear, but very hard to explain. It's practically always in answer to something. You try to get the answer yourself; you struggle hard, and sometimes you don't seem to be able to get through. You think all this is useless; I'm too tense, and at the back of my mind there are other things. You just have to relax, and concentrate. I can get into the state where I say it's just no good. And then suddenly, when you're not expecting it, you're through; the lines are clear, and you get a marvellous answer, absolutely vivid, enormously – I can't describe it – serene, enormous wisdom.

from Edward Robinson, *Living the Questions*

60   I am twelve years old, reading on the window sill in the fruit shed. I am kneeling on a wicker hamper, and my knees are numb. The daylight is cold and cramped . . . I have

read myself out of existence. No such person inhabits the dark day; but suddenly I come awake with a rush of feeling. My crowded head feels suddenly clear, empty and airy as craning out of the window, I look hungrily around. This is real, I think, the colours, the brick, the ivy. It is as though something is going to be shown to me, once and for ever. Things seem so *clear*; they seem to declare themselves aloud. My eyes have touch, my skin on which the air plays seems to be as glass through which I can look from every pore. Awake, awake to all, I know it is a rare moment, perhaps a beginning of a life separate from ordinary existence.

And yet what is there? The elm tree dropping leaves yellow golden all over, into the rainwater tank. They slide slowly downward on the point and settle with the faintest breath of sound on the olive surface. And below them, in the cube of water, like things tranced in ice are others suspended on edge and rotting. Then there is the pipe, and the gray cobwebs stretched across the corners of the tank, and then suddenly the bright shadow of the tree itself with all its stars of sky – lovely but gone almost before it can be lovely.

I lean out, sighing with the strange feeling in me. I can touch the cold sides of the tank; I feel as though I can touch with my mind the tree trunk, the hedge, the hurdle, even the farthest hill that I can see. What are all these familiar things saying so clearly? Why have I never seen them like this before? A moment ago they existed but quietly and without me. Now the leaves keep falling so queerly – queerly as though I had something to do with their falling. Something is happening which makes me able to say and know that it is true: 'I shall remember this. I shall remember each vein on each leaf. I shall be able to see this whenever I want to, wherever I am!'

from Margiad Evans, *Autobiography*

61   . . . And I have felt
        A presence that disturbs me with the joy
        Of elevated thoughts; a sense sublime
        Of something far more deeply interfused,
        Whose dwelling is the light of setting suns,
        And the round ocean and the living air,
        And the blue sky, and in the mind of man;
        A motion and a spirit, that impels

All thinking things, all objects of all thought,
And rolls through all things.

William Wordsworth, 'Lines composed a few miles above Tintern Abbey'

62   she almost saw it once in a rose –
a certain breath of wonder
she looked again perhaps that was her mistake
she should have gone on walking

and then again in mountain country
she heard an echo again
but it was muffled by thunder
and she had no ear for music

In the years that followed she found it again and again
in children that later got arrested on drugs charges
flowers that died, animals that bit her;
she almost had it by the hand in a symphony concert
but even the music faded

and when she finally found it (she was one of the lucky
    ones)
she found it in such a strange manner
it came up behind her and spoke to her
for a time she was frightened but at last she turned
    round

and it knew her, it loved her it spoke her name
it had always known her
it was amazing it was perfect
it was true, at last.

David Porter, 'The Search'

Responding to the personal presence

In the story of Rat and Mole's early morning boat voyage in search of the lost young otter, Kenneth Grahame explores the mixed feelings which people have when they suddenly find themselves in the mysterious presence of their God. Face to face with the God Pan, Rat and Mole experience profound fear and admiration, diffidence and trust.

63   In silence Mole rowed steadily, and soon they came to a point where the river divided, a long backwater branching off to one side. . . .

'Clearer and nearer still,' cried the Rat joyously. 'Now you must surely hear it! Ah – at last – I see you do!'

Breathless and transfixed the Mole stopped rowing as the liquid run of that glad piping broke on him like a wave, caught him up, and possessed him utterly. He saw the tears on his comrade's cheeks, and bowed his head and understood. For a space they hung there, brushed by the purple loosestrife that fringed the bank; then the clear imperious summons that marched hand-in-hand with the intoxicating melody imposed its will on Mole, and mechanically he bent to his oars again. And the light grew steadily stronger, but no birds sang as they were wont to do at the approach of dawn; and but for the heavenly music all was marvellously still.

On either side of them, as they glided onwards, the rich meadow-grass seemed that morning of a freshness and a greenness unsurpassable. Never had they noticed the roses so vivid, the willow-herb so riotous, the meadow-sweet so odorous and pervading. Then the murmur of the approaching weir began to hold the air, and they felt a consciousness that they were nearing the end, whatever it might be, that surely awaited their expedition.

A wide half-circle of foam and glinting lights and shining shoulders of green water, the great weir closed the backwater from bank to bank, troubled all the quiet surface with twirling eddies and floating foam-streaks, and deadened all other sounds with its solemn and soothing rumble.

In midmost of the stream, embraced in the weir's shimmering armspread, a small island lay anchored, fringed close with willow and silver birch and alder. . . .

Slowly, but with no doubt or hesitation whatever, and in something of a solemn expectancy, the two animals passed through the broken, tumultuous water and moored their boat at the flowery margin of the island. In silence they landed, and pushed through the blossom and scented herbage and undergrowth that led up to the level ground, till they stood on a little lawn of marvellous green, set round with Nature's own orchard-trees – crab-apple, wild cherry, and sloe.

'This is the place of my song-dream, the place the music played to me,' whispered the Rat, as if in a trance. 'Here, in this holy place, here if anywhere, surely we shall find Him!'

Then suddenly the Mole felt a great Awe fall upon him, an awe that turned his muscles to water, bowed his head, and rooted his feet to the ground. It was no panic terror – indeed he felt wonderfully at peace and happy – but it was an awe that smote and held him and, without seeing, he knew it could only mean that some august Presence was very, very near. With difficulty he turned to look for his friend, and saw him at his side cowed, stricken, and trembling violently. And still there was utter silence in the populous bird-haunted branches around them; and still the light grew and grew.

Perhaps he would never have dared to raise his eyes, but that, though the piping was now hushed, the call and the summons seemed still dominant and imperious. He might not refuse, were Death himself waiting to strike him instantly, once he had looked with mortal eye on things rightly kept hidden. Trembling he obeyed, and raised his humble head; and then, in that utter clearness of the imminent dawn, while Nature, flushed with fullness of incredible colour, seemed to hold her breath for the event, he looked in the very eyes of the Friend and Helper; saw the backward sweep of the curved horns, gleaming in the growing daylight; saw the stern, hooked nose between the kindly eyes that were looking down on them humorously, while the bearded mouth broke into a half-smile at the corners; saw the rippling muscles on the arm that lay across the broad chest, the long supple hand still holding the pan-pipes only just fallen away from the parted lips; saw the splendid curves of the shaggy limbs disposed in majestic ease on the sward; saw, last of all, nestling between his very hooves, sleeping soundly in entire peace and contentment, the little, round, podgy childish form of the baby otter. All this he saw, for one moment breathless and intense, vivid on the morning sky; and still, as he looked, he lived; and still, as he lived, he wondered.

'Rat!' he found breath to whisper, shaking. 'Are you afraid?'

'Afraid?' murmured the Rat, his eyes shining with unutterable love. 'Afraid! Of Him? O, never, never! And yet – and yet – O, Mole, I am afraid!'

Then the two animals, crouching to the earth, bowed their heads and did worship.

from Kenneth Grahame, *The Wind in the Willows*

The Christian encounter with mystery

For the Christian it is God who is the living presence at the heart of the mystery. The mystery reveals him to be the utterly awesome yet utterly merciful God of Jesus Christ. The record of the prophet Isaiah's call (no. 64), the poem which follows (no. 65), and the parable of the Prodigal Son (no. 66) show what it is like to encounter God in the mystery as the God of majesty and mercy.

64   In the year of King Uzziah's death I saw the Lord seated on a throne, high and exalted, and the skirt of his robe filled the temple. About him were attendant seraphim, and each had six wings; one pair covered his face and one pair his feet, and one pair was spread in flight. They were calling ceaselessly to one another

> Holy, holy, holy is the LORD of Hosts:
>   the whole earth is full of his glory.

And, as each one called, the threshold shook to its foundations, while the house was filled with smoke. Then I cried,

> Woe is me! I am lost,
> for I am a man of unclean lips
> and I dwell among a people of unclean lips;
> yet with these eyes I have seen the King, the LORD of
>   Hosts.

Then one of the seraphim flew to me carrying in his hand a glowing coal which he had taken from the altar with a pair of tongs. He touched my mouth with it and said,

See, this has touched your lips;
your iniquity is removed,
and your sin is wiped away.

Then I heard the Lord saying, Whom shall I send? Who will go
for me? And I answered, Here am I; send me.

Isaiah 6: 1–9a

65   Lord God
I meet you
in the mystery
of life
the sudden silences
intensity of presence
that makes me
stop
catch my breath
lift up head
high
to catch the glory
of your moment

and then
bow
low
lost in the misery of my meagre self

so small
so weak
so far

from you.

God
you are of a grandeur and glory
I long after
and shrink from.

Have mercy!
In your glory
let your pity

touch me.

Nicola Slee, 'Kyrie Eleison'

66   Jesus said, 'A man had two sons. The younger said to his
         father, "Father, let me have the share of the estate that
would come to me." So the father divided the property between
them. A few days later, the younger son got together everything
he had and left for a distant country where he squandered his
money on a life of debauchery.

'When he had spent it all, that country experienced a severe
famine, and now he began to feel the pinch, so he hired himself
out to one of the local inhabitants who put him on his farm to
feed the pigs. And he would willingly have filled his belly with
the husks the pigs were eating but no one offered him anything.
Then he came to his senses and said, "How many of my father's
paid servants have more food than they want, and here am I
dying of hunger! I will leave this place and go to my father and
say; Father, I have sinned against heaven and against you; I no
longer deserve to be called your son; treat me as one of your paid
servants." So he left the place and went back to his father.

'While he was still a long way off, his father saw him and was
moved with pity. He ran to the boy, clasped him in his arms and
kissed him tenderly. Then his son said, "Father, I have sinned
against heaven and against you. I no longer deserve to be called
your son." But the father said to his servants, "Quick! Bring out
the best robe and put it on him; put a ring on his finger and
sandals on his feet. Bring the calf we have been fattening, and
kill it; we are going to have a feast, a celebration, because this
son of mine was dead and has come back to life; he was lost and is
found." And they began to celebrate.

'Now the elder son was out in the fields, and on his way back,
as he drew near the house, he could hear music and dancing.
Calling one of the servants he asked what it was all about. "Your
brother has come" replied the servant "and your father has
killed the calf we had fattened because he has got him back safe
and sound." He was angry then and refused to go in, and his
father came out to plead with him; but he answered his father,
"Look, all these years I have slaved for you and never once
disobeyed your orders, yet you never offered me so much as a kid
for me to celebrate with my friends. But for this son of yours,
when he comes back after swallowing up your property – he and
his women – you kill the calf we had been fattening."

'The father said, "My son, you are with me always and all I

have is yours. But it was only right we should celebrate and
rejoice, because your brother here was dead and has come to life;
he was lost and is found."'

Luke 15: 11–32

The Christian response to the personal presence

Confronted by the mystery of God's love, the Christian's reaction is similar
to that of Rat and Mole (see no. 63) – a mixture of diffidence and
confidence, of fear and trust. Overwhelmed by the God of majesty and
mercy, the Christian responds with adoration and love, fear and trembling.
The following extracts all express this two-fold movement of faith, summed
up most simply in the prayer 'Lord, have mercy', which unites the cry for
mercy with adoration of the Lord whose very nature is to have mercy.

67   Faith is firstly the apprehension of a mystery too great
        for us to understand. We believe in a truth which is
beyond all our own truths. The only proper attitude is to remain
before it in silence, in humility and adoration. . . . It does not
matter if we have little to offer in our prayer, so long as we offer
it humbly. . . . It is an act of faith in the immense mystery of love
in which we are involved, the bowing down of our whole self
before it. In our weakness we must live a mystery infinitely
beyond us but also intimately present to us.

from Georges LeFebvre, 'Lord Stay With Us'

68   Blessed be thou, OLord God,
            in the thousand mysteries of thy Word and will,
            in the thousand, thousand wonders of thy love.
        Let all mortal flesh keep silence
            and lift itself above all earthly thought,
                kneel and adore.

    Eric Milner-White, 'God'

69   Let all mortal flesh keep silence,
        And with fear and trembling stand;
        Ponder nothing earthly-minded,
        For with blessing in his hand

Christ our God to earth descendeth,
Our full homage to demand.

from Liturgy of St James

70   Have mercy
Upon us.
Have mercy
Upon our efforts,
That we
Before Thee,
In love and in faith
Righteousness and humility,
May follow Thee,
With self-denial, steadfastness and courage,
And meet Thee
In the silence.

Give us
A pure heart
That we may know Thee,
A humble heart
That we may hear Thee,
A heart of love
That we may serve Thee,
A heart of faith
That we may live Thee,

Thou
Whom I do not know
But Whose I am

Thou
Whom I do not comprehend
But Who has dedicated me
To my fate.
Thou –

from Dag Hammarskjold, *Markings*

71   Have mercy on me, God, in your kindness.
        In your compassion blot out my offence.
        O wash me more and more from my guilt
        and cleanse me from my sin.

        My offences truly I know them;
        my sin is always before me.
        Against you, you alone, have I sinned;
        what is evil in your sight I have done.

        That you may be justified when you give sentence
        and be without reproach when you judge
        O see, in guilt I was born,
        a sinner was I conceived.

        Indeed you love truth in the heart;
        then in the secret of my heart teach me wisdom
        O purify me, then I shall be clean;
        O wash me, I shall be whiter than snow.

        Make me hear rejoicing and gladness,
        that the bones you have crushed may thrill.
        From my sins turn away your face
        and blot out all my guilt.

        A pure heart create for me, O God,
        put a steadfast spirit within me.
        Do not cast me away from your presence,
        nor deprive me of your holy spirit.

        Give me again the joy of your help;
        with a spirit of fervour sustain me,
        that I may teach transgressors your ways
        and sinners may return to you.

        O rescue me, God my helper,
        and my tongue shall ring out your goodness.
        O Lord, open my lips
        and my mouth shall declare your praise.

For in sacrifice you take no delight,
burnt offering from me you would refuse,
my sacrifice, a contrite spirit.
A humbled, contrite heart you will not spurn.

Psalm 51: 1–17

72   Lord Jesus Christ,
        Son of the living God,
        have mercy on me,
        a sinner.

The Jesus Prayer

73   The Jesus Prayer embraces the two chief 'moments' of
        Christian devotion: the 'moment' of adoration, of look-
ing up to God's glory and reaching out to Him in love; and the
'moment' of penitence, the sense of unworthiness and sin. There
is a circular movement within the Prayer, a sequence of ascent
and return. In the first half of the Prayer we rise up to God: 'Lord
Jesus Christ, Son of God . . .'; and then in the second half we
return to ourselves in compunction: '. . . have mercy on me a
sinner'. . . . These two 'moments' . . . are united and reconciled
in a third 'moment' as we pronounce the word 'mercy'. . . . He
who says to God, 'Have mercy', laments his own helplessness,
but voices at the same time a cry of hope. He speaks not only of
sin but of its overcoming. He affirms that God in his glory
accepts us though we are sinners, asking from us in return to
accept the fact that we are accepted.

from Kallistos Ware, The Power of the Name

74   Let us, then, hold firmly to the faith we profess. For we
        have a great high priest who has gone into the very
presence of God – Jesus, the Son of God. Our high priest is not
one who cannot feel sympathy with our weaknesses. On the
contrary, we have a high priest who was tempted in every way
that we are, but did not sin. Let us be brave, then, and come
forward to God's throne, where there is grace. There we will
receive mercy and find grace to help us just when we need it.

Hebrews 4: 14–16

75   I am here! O my God.
I am here, I am here!
You draw me away from earth,
and I climb to You
in a passion of shrilling,
to the dot in heaven
where, for an instant, You crucify me.
When will You keep me forever?
Must You always let me fall
back to the furrow's dip,
a poor bird of clay?
Oh, at least
let my exultant nothingness
soar to the glory of Your mercy
in the same hope,
until death.   Amen.

Carmen Bernos de Gasztoid, 'The Prayer of the Lark'

4
THE WORLD OF MUSIC

Look at your life: listen to the sounds and music that fill your life. Consider the wonder of music: its power to create new worlds and new visions, to bring happiness and pain. Think of your own response to music: what does it say to you? What does it bring to you?

Look at your life: listen to the music of the whole creation around you, the music of earth, sea and air; the music of animals, birds and human beings.

Look at your life, says the Christian: listen to the whole creation responding in songs of praise to the Creator God. Listen to the music of the Church gathering up praise and penitence, adoration and abjection in songs of worship offered to God.

The beginnings of music

The beginnings of music are shrouded in mystery; the following three passages wonder how and why music may have come into the world. The writers suggest, in different ways, that from the very beginning of things music has been at the heart of our world and at the heart of human experience.

C. S. Lewis describes the magic creation of the world of Narnia through music:

76   In the darkness something was happening. A voice had begun to sing. It was very far away and Digory found it hard to decide from what direction it was coming. Sometimes it seemed to come from all directions at once. Sometimes he almost thought it was coming out of the earth beneath them. Its lower notes were deep enough to be the voice of the earth herself. There were no words. There was hardly even a tune. But it was, beyond comparison, the most beautiful noise he had ever heard. . . .

Then two wonders happened at the same moment. One was that the voice was suddenly joined by other voices; more voices than you could possibly count. They were in harmony with it, but far higher up the scale: cold, tingling, silvery voices. The second wonder was that the blackness overhead, all at once, was blazing with stars. . . . One moment there had been nothing but darkness; next moment a thousand, thousand points of light leaped out – single stars, constellations, and planets, brighter and bigger than any in our world. . . .

The Voice on the earth was now louder and more triumphant; but the voices in the sky . . . began to get fainter. And now something else was happening.

Far away . . . the sky began to turn grey. A light wind, very fresh, began to stir. The sky . . . grew slowly and steadily paler. You could see shapes of hills standing up dark against it. All the time the Voice went on singing. . . .

The eastern sky changed from white to pink and from pink to gold. The Voice rose and rose till all the air was shaking with it. And just as it swelled to the mightiest and most glorious sound it had yet produced, the sun arose.

from C. S. Lewis, *The Magician's Nephew*

77   How and where did music begin?

The fact is that no one knows. . . . From its very beginnings music has been closely identified with the meaning, and the mystery, of life. . . .

The discovery of song and the creation of musical instruments both owed their origin to a human impulse which lies much deeper than conscious intention: the need for rhythm in life. Just as day follows night, the tides advance and recede, the moon waxes and wanes and the seasons succeed one another, so the human organism responds to rhythm. The need is a deep one, transcending thought. . . . Our earliest ancestors were instinctively aware of the need; and so, at a very early date, rhythmic actions and rhythmic songs, together with a growing number of instruments whose voices must themselves have seemed at first mysterious, were used to bring man into contact with the mysteries of life.

from Richard Baker, *The Magic of Music*

78   Da, da, boom boom, da boom,
       da, boom, boom.
          THAT'S THE METRE.
       The what?
          The metre. The rhythm.
       I'm not up on metres, but I sure know
       it has a strong beat.
          Like a heartbeat.
       Like a drum.
          Like clapping thunder.
       Like Mexican castanets.
          Like the rhythm of tidal waves:
       Like the beat of a bass fiddle.
          Like a jumping rope hitting the pavement.
       Like feet tapping and hands beating the table.
       Like a sax and a snare.
          You hear the beat in the sax and fiddle,
          the castanet and the drum.
       You hear the beat in the jumping rope, thunder,
       tidal waves, and heart beat.
          You've got the rhythm of the song.
       I feel it. I've got the rhythm.

Capture the metre, of the clapping thunder.
I'll put it into captivity.
Lock the thunder into the drum.
And the clapping of the jumping rope
on the hot pavement into the castanets.
What's the rhythm of the tidal waves?
The chording of the fiddle.
The piano?
The wind, cutting all the corners of houses
and through the trees.
The heartbeat?
the metronome.
It holds every sound to its metre.
Who made the rhythm of the castanet
and the clapping of thunder?
and the clapping of hands?
And the deep – inside unconscious feel of the beat?
I did. When I made all things,
I made them with a beat.

Herbert Brokering 'Rhythm'

When music speaks

Through their music both composers and players communicate their ideas and feelings. James Baldwin listens to what the saxophone player is saying in his improvised solo (no. 79); then two passages describe how, through their music, Stainer and Messiaen express the horror of the crucifixion (no. 80) and the awe of the resurrection (no. 81).

79   The joint, as Fats Waller would have said, was jumping.
         . . . And during the last set . . . the saxophone player
took off on a terrific solo. He was a kid . . . from some insane
place like Jersey City or Syracuse, but somewhere along the line
he had discovered that he could say it with a saxophone. . . . He
stood there, wide-legged, humping the air, filling his barrel
chest, shivering in the rags of his twenty-odd years, and screaming through the horn *Do you love me? Do you love me? Do you
love me?* And again – *Do you love me? Do you love me? Do you
love me?* The same phrase, unbearably, endlessly, and variously

repeated with all the force the boy had. . . . The question was terrible and real. . . . The men on the stand stayed with him, cool and at a little distance, adding and questioning . . . but each man knew that the boy was blowing for every one of them.

from James Baldwin, *Another Country*

80   On all special occasions the choir would sing cantatas, such as *Elijah* and Stainer's *Crucifixion.* My earliest recollection of feeling the horror of the crucifixion was the music that accompanied one of these cantatas. There is a terrifying organ passage of deep, deep notes somewhere near a passage about 'darkness covered the earth'. Year after year I dreaded yet half yearned to hear it, and feel again this unspeakable suffering and the unimaginable relief of 'It is finished'.

from Edward Robinson, *The Original Vision*

81   Let us begin with Messiaen: the third section of *Et Expecto Resurrectionem Mortuorum.* Woodwinds jump, growl and shriek. Eight solemn bell strokes echo and die. Again silence. Suddenly the brasses blare, and out of the trombones' awesome processional grows a steady roar . . . the big gongs, the tam-tam beaten in a long and powerful resonance, shattering and echoing across mountains and along valleys. This is music of the high hills, music for vast spaces: 'The hour is coming when the dead shall hear the voice of the Son of God.' We can feel the awe and the majesty, the High Alps and the great churches. The instrumental sounds are vast, the silences are deep. The words of St John are alive in the music, and through these sounds Messiaen reveals himself and his vision.

from John Paynter and Peter Aston, *Sound and Silence*

When music sounds

When music sounds a whole new world can be conjured up in the mind of the listener; a world of pictures, images, feelings. Music has the power to soothe – and to hurt.

82   When music sounds, gone is the earth I know,
        And all her lovely things even lovelier grow;
        Her flowers in vision flame, her forest trees
        Lift burdened branches, stilled with ecstasies.

        When music sounds, out of the water rise
        Naiads whose beauty dims my waking eyes
        Rapt in strange dreams burns each enchanted face,
        With solemn echoing stirs their dwelling-place.

        When music sounds, all that I was, I am
        Ere to this haunt of brooding dust I came
        While from Time's Woods break into distant song
        The swift-winged hours, as I hasten along.

        Walter de la Mare 'Music'

83   It was a typical summer evening in June, the atmos-
        phere being in such delicate equilibrium and so trans-
missive that inanimate objects seemed endowed with two or
three senses, if not five. . . . The soundlessness impressed Tess
as a positive entity rather than as the mere negation of noise. It
was broken by the strumming of strings.

        Tess had heard those notes in the attic above her head. Dim,
flattened, constrained by their confinement, they had never
appealed to her as now, when they wandered in the still air with
a stark quality like that of nudity. . . . As she listened Tess, like
a fascinated bird, could not leave the spot. . . .

        Tess was conscious of neither time nor space. The exaltation
which she had described as being producible at will by gazing at
a star, came now without any determination of hers; she undu-
lated upon the thin notes of the second-hand harp, and their
harmonies passed like breezes through her, bringing tears into
her eyes. The floating pollen seemed to be the notes made
visible, and the dampness of the garden the weeping of the
garden's sensibility. Though near nightfall, the rank-smelling

weed-flowers glowed as if they would not close for intentness, and the waves of colour mixed with the waves of sound.

from Thomas Hardy, *Tess of the D'Urbervilles*

84   The spirit of the Lord had forsaken Saul, and at times an evil spirit from the Lord would seize him suddenly. His servants said to him, 'You see, sir, how an evil spirit from God seizes you; why do you not command your servants here to go and find some man who can play the harp? – then, when an evil spirit from God comes on you, he can play and you will recover.' Saul said to his servants, 'Find me a man who can play well and bring him to me.' One of his attendants said, 'I have seen a son of Jesse of Bethlehem who can play; he is a brave man and a good fighter, wise in speech and handsome, and the Lord is with him.' Saul therefore sent messengers to Jesse and asked him to send him his son David. . . . And whenever a spirit from God came upon Saul, David would take his harp and play on it, so that Saul found relief; he recovered and the evil spirit left him alone.

1 Samuel 16: 14–19, 23

85   The radio was on as usual. . . .

One programme came on after another, and all of them were punk. Mick didn't especially care. She smoked and picked a little bunch of grass blades. After a while a new announcer started talking. He mentioned Beethoven. She had read in the library about that musician – his name was pronounced with an *a* and spelled with a double *e*. He was a German fellow like Mozart. When he was living he spoke in a foreign language and lived in a foreign place – like she wanted to do. The announcer said they were going to play his third symphony. She only halfway listened because she wanted to walk some more and she didn't care much what they played. Then the music started. Mick raised her head and her fist went up to her throat.

How did it come? For a minute the opening balanced from one side to the other. Like a walk or a march. Like God strutting in the night. The outside of her was suddenly froze and only that first part of the music was hot inside her heart. She could not even hear what sounded after, but she sat there waiting and froze, with her fists tight. After a while the music came again, harder and loud. It didn't have anything to do with God. This was her, Mick Kelly, walking in the daytime and by herself at night. In the hot sun and in the dark with all the plans and feelings. This music was her – the real plain her.

She could not listen good enough to hear it all. The music boiled inside her. Which? To hang on to certain wonderful parts and think them over so that later she would not forget – or should she let go and listen to each part that came without thinking or trying to remember? . . . The whole world was this music and she could not listen hard enough. Then at last the opening music came again, with all the different instruments bunched together for each note like a hard, tight fist that socked at her heart. And the first part was over.

This music did not take a long time or a short time. It did not have anything to do with time going by at all. She sat with her arms held tight around her legs, biting her salty knee very hard. It might have been five minutes she listened or half the night. The second part was black-coloured – a slow march. Not sad, but like the whole world was dead and black and there was no use thinking back how it was before. One of those horn kind of instruments played a sad and silver tune. Then the music rose up angry and with excitement underneath. And finally the black march again.

But maybe the last part of the symphony was the music she loved the best – glad and like the greatest people in the world running and springing up in a hard, free way. Wonderful music like this was the worst hurt there could be. The whole world was this symphony, and there was not enough of her to listen.

It was over, and she sat very stiff with her arms around her knees. Another programme came on the radio and she put her fingers in her ears. The music left only this bad hurt in her, and a blankness. She could not remember any of the symphony, not even the last few notes. She tried to remember, but no sound at all came to her. Now that it was over there was only her heart like a rabbit and this terrible hurt.

from C. McCullers, *The Heart is a Lonely Hunter*

The whole creation making music

The whole world is alive with music: the music of birds, sea, wind, rain and the animal world, as well as the music made by human beings. The following passages give a rich impression of this great symphony of sound.

86   Oh, the honey-bees are gumming
        On their little wings, and humming
        That the summer, which is coming,
            Will be fun.
        And the cows are almost cooing,
        And the turtle-doves are mooing,
        Which is why a Pooh is poohing
            In the sun.

        For the spring is really springing;
        You can see a skylark singing,
        And the blue-bells, which are ringing,
            Can be heard.
        And the cuckoo isn't cooing,
        But he's cucking and he's ooo-ing,
        And a Pooh is simply poohing
            Like a bird.

A. A. Milne, 'Noise, by Pooh'

87   The silver swan, who living had no note,
        When death approached unlocked her silent throat;
        Leaning her breast against the reedy shore,
        Thus sang her first and last, and sung no more:
        Farewell, all joys; O death, come close mine eyes;
        More geese than swans now live, more fools than wise.

'The silver swan', anonymous (1612)

88   And then I pressed the shell
        Close to my ear.
        And listened well.
        And straightway, like a bell,
        Came low and clear
        The slow, sad murmur of far distant seas
        Whipped by an icy breeze
        Upon a shore

Wind-swept and desolate. . . .
And in the hush of waters was the sound
Of pebbles, rolling round,
For ever rolling, with a hollow sound;
And bubbling sea-weeds, as the waters go
Swish to and fro
Their long, cold tentacles of slimy grey.

James Stephens, 'The Shell'

89   All day I hear the noise of waters
        Making moan
Sad as the seabird is when going
        Forth alone
He hears the wind cry to the waters
        Monotone.

The grey winds, the cold winds are blowing
        Where I go
I hear the noise of many waters
        Far below
All day, all night I hear them flowing
        To and fro.

James Joyce, 'Chamber Music XXXV'

90   In the corner of Crombie's field
the donkey gets madder every minute. I listen
to his heehawing
seesawing and imagine
the round rich note
he wants to propel into space,
a golden planet of sound orbiting
to the wonder of the world.

No wonder
when he hears what comes out of
that whooping-cough trombone
his eyes fill with tears
and his box head drops
to lip the leaves of thistles – accepting that
they're all he deserves.

Norman MacCaig, 'Frustrated Virtuoso'

91   I hear America singing, the varied carols I hear,
         Those of mechanics, each one singing his as it should
             be blithe and strong,
         The carpenter singing his as he measures his plank or
             beam,
         The mason singing his as he makes ready for work, or
             leaves off work,
         The boatman singing what belongs to him in his boat,
             the deck-hand singing on the steamboat deck,
         The shoemaker singing as he sits on his bench, the
             hatter singing as he stands,
         The wood-cutter's song, the ploughboy's on his way in
             the morning, or at noon intermission or at sundown,
         The delicious singing of the mother, or of the young
             wife at work, or of the girl sewing or washing,
         Each singing what belongs to him or her and to none
             else,
         The day what belongs to the day – at night the party of
             young fellows, robust, friendly,
         Singing with open mouths their strong melodious
             songs.

Walt Whitman, 'I hear America singing'

Creation's music offered to God

The first three passages describe the music offered to God by the whole creation at the foundation of the world and at the birth of Christ (nos. 92, 93, 94). In the following two hymns, the Church takes up the chorus, offering songs of adoration to God from the whole created realm (nos. 95, 96).

92   Then from the heart of the tempest Yahweh gave Job
             his answer. He said: . . .
         Where were you when I laid the earth's foundations?
             Tell me, since you are so well informed! . . .
         What supports its pillars at their bases?
             Who laid its cornerstone
         When all the stars of the morning were singing with
             joy,
             and the Sons of God in chorus were chanting praise?

Job 38: 1–7 (abridged)

93   Angels, from the realms of glory,
      Wing your flight o'er all the earth;
      Ye who sang creation's story
      Now proclaim Messiah's birth:
         Come and worship
         Christ the new-born King,
         Come and worship
         Worship Christ the new-born King.

J. Montgomery, 'Angels, from the realms'

94   There were some shepherds in that part of the country
      who were spending the night in the fields, taking care of
their flocks. An angel of the Lord appeared to them, and the
glory of the Lord shone over them. They were terribly afraid, but
the angel said to them, 'Don't be afraid! I am here with good
news for you, which will bring great joy to all the people. This
very day in David's town your Saviour was born – Christ the
Lord! And this is what will prove it to you – you will find a baby
wrapped in strips of cloth and lying in a manger.'
      Suddenly a great army of heaven's angels appeared with the
angel, singing praises to God:

'Glory to God in the highest heaven,
and peace on earth to those with whom he is pleased!'

Luke 2: 8–14

95   New songs of celebration render
         to him who has great wonders done.
      Love sits enthroned in ageless splendour:
         come and adore the mighty one. . . .

      Joyfully, heartily resounding,
         let every instrument and voice
      peal out the praise of grace abounding,
         calling the whole world to rejoice.
      Trumpets and organs, set in motion
         such sounds as make the heavens ring;
      all things that live in earth and ocean,
         make music for your mighty King.

Rivers and seas and torrents roaring,
     honour the Lord with wild acclaim;
mountains and stones look up adoring
     and find a voice to praise his name.

Erik Routley, 'New Songs of Celebration'

96   Bless the Lord all created things:
          sing his praise and exalt him for ever. . . .

     Bless the Lord sun and moon:
          bless the Lord you stars of heaven;

     bless the Lord all rain and dew:
          sing his praise and exalt him for ever.

     Bless the Lord all winds that blow:
          bless the Lord you fire and heat;

     bless the Lord scorching wind and bitter cold:
          sing his praise and exalt him for ever.

     Bless the Lord dews and falling snows:
          bless the Lord you nights and days;

     bless the Lord light and darkness:
          sing his praise and exalt him for ever. . . .

     Bless the Lord you springs:
          bless the Lord you seas and rivers;

     bless the Lord you whales and all that swim in the
          waters:
          sing his praise and exalt him for ever.

     Bless the Lord all birds of the air:
          bless the Lord you beasts and cattle;

     bless the Lord all men on the earth:
          sing his praise and exalt him for ever. . . .

Bless the Lord all men of upright spirit:
    bless the Lord you that are holy and humble in
    heart.

Bless the Father the Son and the Holy Spirit:
    sing his praise and exalt him for ever.

A Song of Creation (abridged)

The Church's music offered to God I

The following passages call upon Christians to worship in music and song, and reflect upon the place of music in worship.

97   Be filled with the Spirit, addressing one another in psalms and hymns and spiritual songs, singing and making melody to the Lord with all your heart, always and for everything giving thanks in the name of our Lord Jesus Christ to God the Father.

Ephesians 5: 18–20

98   Let all the world
in every corner sing,
my God and King!
The church with psalms must shout,
no door can keep them out;
but, above all, the heart
must bear the longest part.
Let all the world
in every corner sing,
my God and King!

George Herbert, 'Let all the world'

99   There is the tendency to speak of 'music *at* worship' rather than the 'music *of* worship'. Music in worship is often considered, as someone has said, in terms of an 'aural lubricant', something done to bridge the gap between one section of the liturgy and another, to fill up silences, to allow the clergy to move from A to B, to create an 'atmosphere', to

'beautify' the liturgy and so on. But the purpose of church music is not to be prosaically functional, nor to be aesthetically or emotionally gratifying to the congregation. It may be so, but to make church music serve such ends is to keep it earth-bound, man-centred. . . .

The music of worship, truly understood, is always God-centred and God-directed. But this vertical dimension explodes horizontally to draw all the worshippers together. The music of worship is not merely notes and sounds. It is essentially an expression of heart and mind as, filled with the Spirit, the people of God address one another in psalms and hymns and spiritual songs, singing and making melody to the Lord with all their hearts (Ephesians 5:19). Such music is an expression of our faith in God in Christ. . . .

from Robin Leaver, 'Music in church today'

100   Alleluia!
Praise God in his Temple on earth,
praise him in his temple in heaven,
praise him for his mighty achievements,
praise him for his transcendent greatness!

Praise him with blasts of the trumpet,
praise him with lyre and harp,
praise him with drums and dancing,
praise him with strings and reeds,
praise him with clashing cymbals,
praise him with clanging cymbals!
Let everything that breathes praise Yahweh!
Alleluia!

Psalm 150

101   'Times have changed from the times they used to be,'
said Mail. . . . 'I've been thinking we must be almost the last left in the country of the old string players? Barrel-organs, and the things next door to 'em that you blow wi' your foot, have come in terribly of late years.'. . .

'More's the pity,' replied another. 'Time was – long and merry ago now! – when not one of the varmints was to be heard of; but it served some of the quires right. They should have stuck to strings as we did and kept out clarinets, and done away with serpents.* If you'd thrive in musical religion, stick to strings, says I.'

'Strings be safe soul-lifters, as far as that do go,' said Mr Spinks. . . .

'Clar'nets, however, be bad at all times,' said Michael Mail. 'One Christmas . . . I went the rounds wi' the Weatherbury quire. 'Twas a hard frosty night, and the keys of all the clar'nets froze – ah, they did freeze! – so that 'twas like drawing a cork every time a key was opened; and the players o' em had to go into a hedger-and-ditcher's chimley-corner and thaw their clar'nets every now and then. . .'.

'I can well bring back to my mind,' said Mr Penny, 'what I said to poor Joseph Ryme . . . when they thought of having clar'nets there. "Joseph" I said says I, "depend upon't, if so be you have them tooting clar'nets you'll spoil the whole set-out. Clar'nets were not made for the service of the Lord; you can see it by looking at 'em," I said. . .'.

'As far as look is concerned,' said the tranter, 'I don't for my part see that a fiddle is much nearer heaven than a clar'net. 'Tis further off. There's always a rakish, scampish twist about a fiddle's looks that seems to say the wicked one had a hand in making o'en: while angels be supposed to play clar'nets in heaven or som'at like 'em if ye may believe picters.'

'Robert Penny, you was in the right,' broke in the eldest Dewy. 'They should ha' stuck to strings. . . . I don't care who hears me say it, nothing will spak to your heart wi' the sweetness o' the man of strings!'

'Strings for ever!' said Little Jimmy.

'Strings alone would have held their ground against all the new-comers in creation.' ('True, true!' said Bowman.) 'But clarinets was death.' ('Death they was!' said Mr Penny.) 'And harmonions,' William continued in a louder voice, and getting excited by these signs of approval, 'harmonions and barrel-organs' ('Ah!' and groans from Spinks) 'be miserable – what shall I call 'em? – miserable –'

'Sinners,' suggested Jimmy . . .

'Miserable dumbledores!'†

'Right, William, and so they be – miserable dumbledores!' said the choir with unanimity.

from Thomas Hardy, *Under the Greenwood Tree*
* *serpents:* a bass wind-instrument with serpentine bends.
† *dumbledores:* bumble-bees.

102   Music can bring something ... very specific to the
        celebration [of communion]. Just as images ought to
make us contemplate the invisible, so should music enable us to
hear the unheard. I see two ways ... of attaining this.

The first lies in the sound signals which we have not heard
before, which astonish us, wrench us out of the familiar or the
academic and turn our minds toward new spaces of the spirit.
Couldn't contemporary music do this? ...

The second special service could be by the kind of music not
necessarily too difficult to perform, but so suited to what it is
celebrating that it would be an inexhaustible source of prayer,
meaning and feeling. A very simple and pure symbol, like the
water of baptism, the candle flame, the broken bread. A music
that was not full of itself but the bearer of silence and worship as
Mary bore the incarnate Word.

from Joseph Gelineau, *The Liturgy Today and Tomorrow*

The Church's music offered to God II

The music offered by the Church to God varies enormously from tradition
to tradition and from place to place. The following extracts describe the
variety of music to be found in a Russian orthodox (no. 103), a Trappist (no.
104) and a Benedictine monastery (no. 105), and, finally, an experimental
celebration in an American discotheque (no. 106).

103   I set off in a taxi out of Moscow to the Monastery of the
        Old Believers on the outskirts of the city. . . .

I arrived at nine in the morning when the service had obvi-
ously been going on for some time and I left at midday when it
was still going on.

The service itself was very active and, although the priests
conducted most of the action with processions of sacred books
and objects, readings and intonings, etc., the congregation was
also involved. They crossed themselves violently and rhyth-
mically in multiples of three, sometimes never stopping, and
sang the responses to the great antiphons of the Orthodox
liturgy.

The intoned 'reading' from the Bible was, I found, the most
remarkable musical experience. The priest with his long black

hair, huge beard and glittering robes, sang verses from the Bible on one note, as in our psalm-chanting and then slowly rose a semitone or even a quarter tone, in a series of very gradual and almost imperceptible steps. One's ears became keenly attuned to this slow movement upwards – I suppose it has parallels with the movement of incense and spiritual ascent – so that when the final note is reached the sense of resolution and release makes a great climax.

Half-way through the morning a mixed peasant choir, mostly dressed in embroidered white clothes and scarves came into the central body of the church to sing special Christmas hymns. They did not have individual copies of the music but one of the choir held up an enormous book on which great square notes of the hymn appeared. The leader of the group conducted with a three-foot long baton, almost seeming to point out the notes. It was like being flung back to the Middle Ages, I had seen pictures like this in illuminated manuscripts, and here it was going on not five miles from the Russian Space Museum and Exhibition of Twentieth Century Technology.

Ian Barton 'Christmas Day Mass in a Russian Monastery – 6 January 1973'

104   The cold stones of the Abbey church ring with a chant
        that glows with living flame, with clean, profound de-
sire. It is an austere warmth, the warmth of Gregorian chant. It is deep beyond ordinary emotion, and that is one reason why you never get tired of it. . . .

That first evening in choir I tried to sing my first few notes of Gregorian chant with the worst cold I had ever had in my life. . . . Presently the cantor intoned the lovely Advent hymn, Conditor Alme Siderum.

What measure and balance and strength there is in the simplicity of that hymn . . . That evening I saw how the mea-sured tone took the old words of St Ambrose and infused into them even more strength and suppleness and conviction and meaning than they already had and made them flower before God in beauty and in fire, flower along the stones and vanish in the darkness of the vaulted ceiling. And their echo died and left our souls full of peace and grace.

When we began to chant the Magnificat I almost wept, but that was because I was new in the monastery. And in fact it was

precisely because of that that I had reason to weep with thanks-
giving and happiness as I croaked the words in my dry, hoarse
throat, in gratitude for my vocation, in gratitude that I was
really there at last, really in the monastery, and chanting God's
liturgy with His monks.

from Thomas Merton, *The Seven Storey Mountain*

105   The bell began ringing in my dream, a sweet unintru-
       sive pealing, distant and melodious. But as the dream
faded I knew the bell was sounding just outside my window, that
Brother Richard in his plaid jacket and Levi's was pulling the
cord, and that in ten minutes, at 4.30 a.m., the monks would be
gathering for matins.

O sing unto the Lord a new song:
Sing unto the Lord, all the earth,
Sing unto the Lord, bless his name;
Show forth his salvation from day to day.

Without allowing myself the time to decide whether I wanted
to get up or not, I rolled out of bed, sloshed cold water from the
basin on my face, and pulled on my clothes. My visitor's cell in
the Weston priory, following the explicit directions of St Bene-
dict's Rule itself, was scantily but adequately furnished with a
cot, chair, table, lamp, closet, sink and crucifix. Little to distract.
It was February in Vermont, and cold. I put on heavy socks and a
wool sweater and picked my way down-stairs to the simple
common room where the earliest prayers of the day would be
sung.

When I got to the room, most of the tiny monastery's sixteen
monks were already there, sitting quietly on cushions in a
semicircle near the huge picture window. Along the edge of the
darkened hills across a valley, the gray light of the new day was
just beginning to appear. Now one monk struck a chord on his
guitar. Together they all sang, in perfect harmony, to a modern
tune.

Calm is the night, O Lord
    as we wait for you.
All the stars are laughing
    at our wonder.

For a moment I felt utterly at home – with myself, with the monks and with the universe. For a millennium and a half Benedictine monks have been greeting the morning with songs of praise. Here a steel-string guitar, Zen-type cushions and a melody reminiscent of Judy Collins had been added to an ancient ritual with no apparent incongruence. After the prayers and psalms we returned to our cells for a period of individual prayer, then gathered for a silent breakfast, then proceeded to the work of the day.

from Harvey Cox, *Turning East*

106   Two years ago a group of friends and students joined me to organize a celebration of what we called Byzantine Easter in a huge discotheque called The Boston Tea Party. . . . We scheduled the occasion for four in the morning and suggested that those who came should bring a loaf of bread to share. . . .

By three-thirty a.m. the discotheque was already teeming with people, heavy on youth but spanning the alleged generation gap. We had placed a huge table in the middle of the dance floor as an altar. As people arrived they heaped it high with pumpernickel, cinnamon buns, doughnuts, twinkies, long French loaves, matzos, scones, heavy black bread and raisin tarts. . . . By four there were nearly two thousand people present, creating their own cathedral and costuming one another for the rite.

At four-thirty the Passion Week portion of the evening-morning began. Everyone grew serious as a multiscreen light-and-music collage transformed the Tea Party into a contemporary Via Crucis, with scenes of war, death, cruelty, loneliness and racism. People watched and listened intently, singing with the music when they knew it. Then an extraordinary group of free-wheeling liturgical dancers dressed in black and white leotards began to move among the multitudes enticing them into sacred gesture and ritual motion. People who had never danced in their lives before stretched out arms and flexed legs and torsos. The lithe solemnity of the movements made me think we should get rid of pews in churches forever.

After the dancing, people came together in small groups to prepare for the ceremony of the Mass. Hands reached out and clots of people, from three to fifteen, formed. . . . In one group a teeny began humming 'Jesus Loves Me', and soon her whole arm-and-leg-enmeshed group began to hum with her. Then from the sound system poured forth the recitatives and choruses of Bach's St Matthew Passion. Again people clasped and unclasped in embraces; arms reached up and out. 'He was wounded for our iniquities. . . .' The whole crowd seemed to be participating imaginatively in the crucifixion, and in man's perpetual crucifixion of his neighbor.

Then came silence. Then a brief reading from the Gospel of Luke: 'Why seek ye the living among the dead? He is not here, but is risen.' Then Handel's 'Hallelujah' chorus.

It was the high point. Most people have always secretly longed for a chance to sing the 'Hallelujah' chorus, booming out the bass or soprano with full fortissimo. But in our spectator-performer style churches they have mostly had to bite their lips and listen. Here everyone joined in: 'And he shall reign forever and ever . . . .' Not only did they sing, they jumped, danced, applauded. As the last Amen of the chorus faded, the procession entered. It included not only the officiants but a line of fruit and bread and wine bearers, censers and a crucifer, accompanied by the march music from Z. Slowly it wound through the crowd to the bread-bedecked table. Candles flickered, vestments glistened and clouds of incense wafted through the air. . . .

As the ecumenical communion began, an alert quiet crept over the crowd. They joined in the chanting of the Kyrie eleison; they responded to the reading of the prophecy of God's judgement on Babylon with shouts and applause; they hummed a long 'Om' during the epiklesis. Then the celebrants lit the enormous Easter Candle, holding it aloft to the four corners of the earth, blessed the mounds of bread, and invited people to take it 'for free' and share it with their neighbors.

After the benediction we greeted one another with the Kiss of Peace. Again the discotheque swayed and sang. A Resurrection light collage leaped onto the walls. Since the hall is equipped with twenty-six projectors, the effect was like moving in an instant from a dim cave into a cathedral of luminous windows. Just as the collage was reaching its apex with the Beatles singing, 'Here Comes the Sun', someone threw open the back door. By some miracle of celestial timing, the sun was just beginning to peek over the Boston extension of the Massachusetts Turnpike.

from Harvey Cox, *The Seduction of the Spirit*

Appendix 1 SUGGESTIONS FOR DISCUSSION AND ACTIVITIES

1 MEETINGS AND ENCOUNTERS

Discussion

1 In Mig Holder's poem (no. 1), who were the characters? What was the reason for the visit? Was it successful? What makes the meeting in Vivienne Stapley's poem (no. 3) so different?

2 What kind of meeting takes place in e.e. cummings' poem (no. 4)? Why did it have such a profound effect upon the poet?

3 Compare the three poems by Mig Holder, Vivienne Stapley and e.e. cummings (nos. 1, 3, 4). Discuss them in the light of your own experiences of meeting people.

4 What do you notice about other people at a first meeting? What do you look for? What kind of first impressions do you make on others? Are first impressions to be trusted?

5 What makes meeting others difficult? Why do some people experience greater difficulty than others? How can such problems be overcome?

6 What reasons do people give for finding it difficult to 'meet with God'? What answers could Christians give?

7 What does Michel Quoist mean when he talks of meeting God in others (nos. 10, 11)?

8 In the Emmaus story (nos. 14, 15) the disciples did not at first recognise Jesus – why? Why did they recognise him at the meal? What do you think Luke wants his readers to understand by this story?

9 How do you think Christians meet God today (see nos. 16–21)? How can churches help or hinder this meeting?

Activities

1 Choose some of the meetings described in the poems and passages. Act out the situations and develop them using role-play.

2 In pairs explore by role-play what happens in the following situations. One of you should adopt a constant role, and observe how your reactions change to the new role of your partner:
   a) you visit an elderly relative in hospital;
   b) you meet a friend on a bus;
   c) a teacher stops you in the corridor to talk about homework;
   d) a stranger stops you in the street to ask your directions to the railway station.
   Notice especially how your language and gestures change. Why? Invent more roles and act them out.

3 Create a file on meetings which shows how influential they are in shaping our lives. Include important historical and political meetings (from books and newspapers) as well as meetings which have been important in your own life.
4 Using role-play, interview some of the other characters in the New Testament besides Cleopas who met and knew Jesus. What effect did he have upon their lives? How did they respond to their meeting with Jesus? You might try interviewing Peter, Pilate, Mary Magdalene, Nicodemus and Herod.
5 Write a story or a play based on a meeting which has a dramatic effect upon the characters' lives.

2   THE SYMBOL OF WATER

Discussion

1 In what ways do we depend upon water in our daily lives? Discuss problems faced in countries where drought is common. (See nos. 22, 23.)
2 Why do you think poets have found water such a fascinating subject to write about? What aspects of water do the poets in nos 24–30 bring out? How can water become 'an image of myself' (J. de Rooy, no. 24)?
3 The Sikh hymn (no. 31) and the Fisherman's Prayer (no. 32) compare God with a mighty river and the sea. What effect does this produce? What does it say about God and about the worshipper's attitude to God?
4 How does Michel Quoist use the image of water in his poem 'The Sea' (no. 35)?
5 What do the two myths about the flood symbolise (nos. 36, 37)? Compare the biblical story and the story from the Epic of Gilgamesh. (The whole of the biblical story can be found in Genesis chapters 6–9). How are the two stories different?
6 Why is crossing or passing through water a powerful religious symbol? (See nos. 39–42.)
7 What do you think the miracle story in Luke 8: 22–25 (no. 42) would have meant to the first Christians who passed this story on to each other? What does it say to modern Christians?
8 Why are Christians baptised? (See nos. 43–50.) How does baptism represent 'a dying to self and a being reborn to a new life in Christ' (Alan Richardson, no. 48)? Why do you think Jesus was baptised (no. 43)? What are the differences between adult baptism and infant baptism (see nos. 45, 46)?

9 Why is water such an important religious symbol (see nos. 51, 52)? Discuss the different ways in which water is used in the religious stories and rites described in the unit.
10 What does Jesus mean by saying that he will give his disciples 'living water' (nos. 53, 54)?

Activities

1 Produce a file (individually or in groups) entitled 'Water: a necessity of life' showing how all of life is dependent on water.
2 Collect pictures and photographs of water in its many different forms: rain, river, springs, etc. Make a display of them.
3 Observe closely a particular water formation – waves on a shore, rain on a window, a puddle, even a dripping tap. Take time to watch and listen very carefully to details of shape, colour, texture, movement and sound. Create a poem, description or painting on the basis of what you have seen.
4 Read through a service of baptism and, if possible, attend a baptism. Find out how different denominations practise baptism.
5 Using a concordance, look up some of the passages in the Bible about water, and see how it is used in different ways.
6 On the basis of the scripture extracts in no. 53, write a poem or prayer based on water as a symbol of the new life God offers in Jesus.
7 Using any of the material from this project, create a twenty minute period of meditation or reflection on 'the symbol of water'. This could include poems, pictures, music, prayers and scripture passages.

3   THE PRESENCE OF MYSTERY

Discussion

1 What produces the sense of wonder in the poems by Walt Whitman (no. 55) and Norman MacCaig (no. 56)? Compare the two poems.
2 How would you describe and account for Fabien's feelings in the passage from *Night Flight* (no. 57)?
3 The young Wordsworth's lonely adventure (no. 58) left him with 'a dim and undetermined sense of unknown modes of being'. What does this mean? Why did his adventure have this effect upon him?
4 Do you identify with any of the experiences recorded in no. 59, 'Living the Questions'? Why do some people have such experiences whilst others do not?

5 'What are all these familiar things saying so clearly? Why have I never seen them like this before?' (no. 60). Why do familiar things suddenly take on new significance which we have not seen before?

6 'Awake, awake to all, I know it is a rare moment . . .' (no. 60). How can we be awake and responsive to the mystery around us?

7 Wordsworth's 'Tintern Abbey' (no. 61) and David Porter's 'The Search' (no. 62) both describe a presence in the mystery. Is it the same presence in the two poems? If not, what is the difference?

8 'Afraid!' says Rat, 'Of *Him*? O, never, never! And yet – and yet – O, Mole, I am afraid!' (no. 63) What does he mean?

9 How does the Christian respond to meeting God in the mystery? (See nos. 64–75.)

10 The Jesus Prayer (no. 72) is used by millions of Christians because it expresses profoundly the heart of the Christian faith. How does it do this?

11 How can the Christian both adore and fear God?

Activities

1 Think back through your life and recall any occasions when you were aware of mystery. Describe and analyse as precisely as possible your feelings and thoughts on these occasions, and what gave rise to them.

2 Visit impressive countryside, or look for a fine sunset or clear moonlit night. Try to be quiet and alone. Find a spot where you can see as much as possible, and let the grandeur of the place speak to you. Jot down your thoughts and feelings. Later these can be developed into a poem, a prayer or a diary account.

3 Visit a cathedral, abbey or ruined castle. Find out as much as possible about the history, the architecture, the lives of the people who built it. Collect postcards or photographs, and write an account of your visit. What feelings were evoked?

4 Devise a choral or dramatic reading of Psalm 51 (no. 71). Mime or dance could be added, or appropriate music.

5 Explore the two-fold movement of the Jesus Prayer described by Kallistos Ware (no. 73). This can be done in several ways. Use the Jesus Prayer (no. 72) as the basic framework for a poem; draw or paint the words graphically or pictorially; create a dance-movement to express the approach and retreat, the adoration and the fear summed up by the prayer.

6 Think back through your life and recall any occasions when you were aware of the presence of God. What gave rise to these feelings, and how did you respond to them? What does it feel like when you think back over them? Try to express this in words or pictures.

7 Create a thirty minute presentation of slides, music and readings on the theme 'The Presence of Mystery'.

4   THE WORLD OF MUSIC

Discussion

1 Why do you think human beings have a need for rhythm in life? How do we find it? (See nos. 76–78.)
2 Why does music say different things to different people? Can we know what the composer or performer intends us to hear?
3 How can music have the power to both soothe and hurt? Compare the effect of music upon Tess (no. 83) and Mick (no. 85).
4 What sorts of music do you like to listen to or perform? Why?
5 What makes some sounds musical and others not? How can the sound of the sea (see nos. 88, 89) or the donkey's heehawing (see no. 90) be described as music?
6 The books of Job (no. 92) and Luke (no. 94) tell of an angelic choir which greeted the foundation of the world and the birth of Christ. What do you think this signifies?
7 What reasons do nos. 97–102 give for using music in worship? Are there certain sorts of music more suited to church use than others? Should the music be for everyone, or for specially trained musicians?
8 What does Joseph Gelineau (no. 102) mean when he says that music should enable us to hear the unheard?
9 What experiences of music used in worship have you had? Did the music play an important part? Was it successful or not?
10 What does the music contribute to the worship situations described in nos. 103–6?

Activities

1 Make a list of the sounds you are likely to hear in any one day. Which of them are music and why? A tape could be produced of 'A Day's Music'.
2 Choose a particular piece of music from the world of nature – bird song, wind in fir trees, sea on the shore, etc – and try to reproduce the sound as exactly as possible with musical instruments or voices. Or write a 'sound-poem' which tries to capture the exact quality of the sound.
3 Make a list of your favourite pieces of music. Try to analyse why you like them, and what effect they have upon you.

4 Listen to a selection of short pieces of music: a variety of pop, jazz, folk, classical and so on. As each piece is played, jot down the 'pictures' and 'stories' that come to mind. Compare the differences between each piece of music, and between different people's impressions.

5 Using the same short extracts of music, create a sequence of dance and movement which expresses your reactions to the music.

6 Make a group collage of the Song of Creation (no. 96) showing how each part of the creation in its own way sings God's praise and exalts him for ever.

7 Create a group chant of Psalm 150 (no. 100) or the Song of Creation (no. 96) using a leader and a large group, or several smaller groups, or two equal-sized groups. Experiment with using a chorus, repeating short phrases and words, and with different rhythms, volumes, speed and tone of voice.

8 Write a revised 'modern' version of Psalm 150 using modern instruments and your own choice of style. This could be set to music.

9 Make a study of a particular aspect of church music that interests you: organ music, choral works, plainsong, negro spirituals, modern folk hymns, etc.

10 Plan and arrange the music for a special celebration of the Eucharist, paying attention to the way the music enhances the words and actions of the liturgy.

Appendix 2   SUGGESTED COLLECTS AND READINGS FOR USE IN THE CELEBRATION OF COMMUNION

1   MEETINGS AND ENCOUNTERS

This unit can be used with the first unit in *His Spirit is With Us* to explore the opening Greeting of the communion service.

First reading: Ruth 2: 1–12

Second reading: Acts 2: 42–47

Gospel reading: Luke 24: 13–35

Collect:

Lord Jesus Christ, risen Lord,
you met your disciples on the road to Emmaus;
you made yourself known to them
    when you broke the bread.
Make yourself known to us now
    as we meet with you in the breaking of bread.
For you are our God for ever and ever.   Amen.

2   THE SYMBOL OF WATER

This unit can be used with the second unit in *His Spirit is With Us* to explore the Collect for Purity in the communion service.

First reading: Genesis 7: 17–23

Second reading: Acts 8: 35–39

Gospel reading: Mark 1: 1–13

Collect:

Almighty God,
you sent your servant John
    to cleanse your people with the water of baptism
    and to prepare them for the coming of your Son.
Send now your Holy Spirit upon us
    to cleanse the thoughts of our hearts
    and to prepare us for his coming in the eucharist,
who is alive and reigns
    with you and the Holy Spirit,
    one God, now and for ever.   Amen.

3 THE PRESENCE OF MYSTERY

This unit can be used with the third unit in *His Spirit is With Us* to explore the Kyrie in the communion service.

First reading: Psalm 51: 1–17 or Isaiah 6: 1–9a

Second reading: Hebrews 4: 14–16

Gospel reading: Luke 15: 11–32

Collect:
> Lord God,
> you meet us in the mysteries of life
> and the wonder of creation.
> Open our eyes
> to the mystery of your presence
> and make us confident to draw near you
> in your holiness and mercy;
> through Jesus Christ our Lord.   Amen.

4 THE WORLD OF MUSIC

This unit can be used with the fourth unit in *His Spirit is With Us* to explore the Gloria in the communion service.

First reading: Psalm 150

Second reading: Ephesians 5: 18–20

Gospel reading: Luke 2: 8–14

Collect:
> Lord God,
> you have created rhythm and melody
> at the heart of your world
> and in the heart of your people.
> Open our ears
> to hear the music of your creation.
> Open our hearts
> to respond to the music of your love.
> Open our mouths
> to make music to your praise and glory;
> in the name of Jesus Christ our Lord.   Amen.

SOURCES OF READINGS

Note: Sources are listed here, whether copyright or not, to facilitate further reference. Permission to reproduce copyright material is gratefully acknowledged.

1 Mig Holder, 'Question', *Making Eden Grow*, Scripture Union, London, 1974, p. 13
2 Kathy, 'Words', *Dare to Live: Taizé 1974, Preparing for the World-wide Council of Youth*, SPCK, London, 1973, p. 108. Used by permission of SPCK and Les Presses de Taizé
3 Vivienne Stapley, 'To L', *Making Eden Grow*, op cit, p. 31
4 e. e. cummings, *73 poems*, Faber and Faber, London, 1974
5 Sheldon Vanauken, *A Severe Mercy*, Hodder and Stoughton, London, 1977, pp. 24–5. Used by permission
6 Ruth 2: 1–12, *New English Bible*, Oxford and Cambridge University Press, 2nd edition © 1970. Used by permission
7 Lewis Carroll, *Through the Looking Glass*, Penguin Books, Harmondsworth, 1962, pp. 267–9
8 Elizabeth Goudge, *The Herb of Grace*, Hodder and Stoughton, London, 1965, pp. 41–2. Used by permission of David Higham Associates
9 Norman Habel, 'I feel such a fool trying to believe', *Interrobang*, Lutterworth, London, 1970, pp. 13–14. Used by permission
10 Michel Quoist, *The Christian Response*, Gill and Macmillan, Dublin, 1965, pp. 95–7. Used by permission
11 Michel Quoist, 'My friend', *Prayers of Life*, Gill and Macmillan, Dublin, 1963, p. 17. Used by permission
12 Roger Bush, 'The Darkened Church', *Prayers for Pagans*, Hodder and Stoughton, London, 1968. Used by permission of Curtis Brown (Aust) Pty Ltd
13 Matthew 25: 34–40, *New English Bible*, op cit
14 Luke 24: 13–35, *Jerusalem Bible*, © 1966, 1967, 1968 Darton, Longman and Todd, London, and Doubleday and Co. Inc. Used by permission
15 Stuart Jackman, *The Davidson Affair*, Faber and Faber, London, 1970, pp. 164–9. Used by permission of Faber and Faber
16 Acts 9:1–8, *New English Bible*, op cit
17 Peter Marshall, *Mr Jones, Meet the Master*, Fontana Books, London, 1964, p. 135
18 Karol, 'He Comes', *Dare to Live: Taizé 1974*, op cit, pp. 68–9. Used by permission of SPCK and Les Presses de Taizé
19 Isabelle, 'Meditation for our Journey', *Dare to Live: Taizé 1974*, op cit, pp. 121–2. Used by permission of SPCK and Les Presses de Taizé
20 Acts 2:42–47, *New English Bible*, op cit
21 Joseph Gelineau, *The Liturgy Today and Tomorrow*, Darton, Longman and Todd, London, 1978, pp. 26–7. Used by permission
22 Debbie Taylor, 'Pure and simple', *New Internationalist*, no. 103, September 1981. Used by permission

23 'People, Water and Ways of Life', *New Internationalist*, no. 103, September 1981. Used by permission

24 J. de Rooy, *Tools for Meditation*, Grail Publications, Pinner, 1976, pp. 23–5. Used by permission

25 James Reeves, 'The Sea', *The Wandering Moon*, William Heinemann, London, 1950, pp. 67–70. Used by permission

26 *Gerard Manley Hopkins: Poems and Prose*, selected and edited by W. H. Gardner, Penguin Books, Harmondsworth, 1953, p. 130

27 Geeta Mohanty, 'Pearls on the grass', in Barry Maybury, *Wordscapes*, Oxford University Press, Oxford, 1970, p. 40

28 Charles Tomlinson, 'During Rain', *Written on Water*, Oxford University Press, London, 1972, pp. 48–9. Used by permission

29 H.D., 'Oread', *Imagist Poetry*, Penguin Books, Harmondsworth, 1972, p. 62. Hilda Doolittle, *Collected Poems of H.D.*, copyright 1925, 1953, by Norman Holmes Pearson. Reprinted by permission of New Directions Publishing Corporation

30 H.D., 'The Pool', *Imagist Poetry*, op cit, p. 67

31 A Sikh hymn quoted in Denys Thompson, *Readings*, Cambridge University Press, Cambridge, 1974, p. 53

32 'The Fisherman's Prayer', quoted in Barbara Greene and Victor Gollancz, *God of a Hundred Names*, Hodder and Stoughton, London, 1962, p. 69

33 Psalm 42: 1–2, *Jerusalem Bible*, op cit

34 Sonia Syner, *Relaxation*, Hillside Press, Caterham, 1978

35 Michel Quoist, 'The Sea', *Prayers of Life*, Gill and Macmillan, 1963, pp. 33–4. Used by permission

36 Genesis 7: 10–8:4, *New English Bible*, op cit

37 N. K. Saunders, *The Epic of Gilgamesh*, Penguin Books, Harmondsworth, 1960, pp. 107–8

38 Rex Chapman, 'The Chaotic Flood', *Out of the Whirlwind*, SCM, London, 1971, p. 5. Used by permission

39 Richard Adams, *Watership Down*, Penguin Books, Harmondsworth, 1973, pp. 41–5 passim. Used by permission of David Higham Associates Ltd

40 F. W. Dillistone, *Christianity and Symbolism*, Collins, London, 1955, pp. 197–8. Used by permission

41 Psalm 136, *The Psalms: a new translation for worship*, Collins, London, 1977

42 Luke 8:22–25, *Revised Standard Version*

43 Mark 1:1–13, *Jerusalem Bible,* op cit

44 Acts 8:35–39, *Good News Bible*, Collins and the Bible Societies, London and Glasgow, 1976. © American Bible Society. Used by permission

45 'The Baptist Deacon' in Ronald Blythe, *Akenfield: Portrait of an English Village*, Penguin Books, Harmondsworth, 1972, pp. 72–4. Used by permission of David Higham Associates Ltd

46 Colin Buchanan, 'Initiation Services', *Anglican Worship Today*, Collins, London, 1980, pp. 152–5

47 The Baptism Service, *The Alternative Service Book 1980.* Copyright © The Central Board of Finance of the Church of England. Used by permission

48 Alan Richardson, *A Dictionary of Christian Theology*, SCM, London, 1969, p. 170

49 John Chrysostom (c 347–407), from *Homily 25 on the Gospel of St John*

50 Norman Habel, 'Born Free: A Baptismal Shout', *Hi! Have a Nice Day*, Lutterworth, Guildford, 1972, p. 68

51 Thomas Fawcett, *The Symbolic Language of Religion*, SCM, London, 1970, pp. 28–9. Used by permission

52 Mircea Eliade, *Patterns in Comparative Religion*, Sheed and Ward, London, 1976, pp. 188–193, passim

53 Isaiah 41:17–18; 44:3–4; 48:21; John 4:13–14, *Jerusalem Bible*, op cit

54 Horatius Bonar (1808–89), 'I heard the voice of Jesus say', in many hymn books

55 Walt Whitman, 'Miracles' *Leaves of Grass*, New York University Press, New York, 1965, pp. 388–9

56 Norman MacCaig, 'An Ordinary Day', *Surroundings*, The Hogarth Press, London, 1966, p. 33. Used by permission of Chatto and Windus Ltd

57 Antoine de Saint-Exupéry, *Night Flight*, Penguin Books, Harmondsworth, 1976, pp. 111–13. Used by permission of William Heinemann Ltd

58 William Wordsworth, *The Prelude* (composed between 1799 and 1805), Penguin Books, Harmondsworth, 1971, pp. 55–7

59 Edward Robinson, *Living the Questions*, The Religious Experience Research Unit, Oxford, 1978, pp. 47, 75–6, 66–7. Used by permission

60 Margiad Evans, *Autobiography*, Basil Blackwell, Oxford, 1943, p. 78

61 William Wordsworth, 'Lines composed a few miles above Tintern Abbey 13 July 1798', *Lyrical Ballads*, Collins, London, 1968, pp. 140–1

62 David Porter, 'The Search', *Making Eden Grow*, op cit, p. 23

63 Kenneth Grahame, *The Wind in the Willows*, Methuen, London, 1961, pp. 132–6

64 Isaiah 6:1–9a, *New English Bible*, op cit

65 Nicola Slee, 'Kyrie Eleison', unpublished

66 Luke 15:11–32, *Jerusalem Bible*, op cit

67 Georges LeFebvre, 'Lord Stay with Us', in Anthony Bloom and Georges LeFebvre, *Courage to Pray*, Darton, Longman and Todd, London, 1973, pp. 105–6

68 Eric Milner-White, 'God', *My God My Glory*, SPCK, London, 1954, p. 83

69 Liturgy of St James, (c. 5th century) translated by G. Moultrie as 'Let all mortal flesh keep silence', in many hymn books

70 Dag Hammarskjold, *Markings*, Faber and Faber, London, 1966, p. 176. Used by permission of Faber and Faber Ltd

71 Psalm 51:1–17, *The Psalms: A New Translation*, Collins, London, 1963. Used by permission of The Grail, England

72 The Jesus Prayer, traditional

73 Kallistos Ware, *The Power of the Name*, SLG Press, Fairacres, 1977, pp. 8–9

74 Hebrews 4:14–16, *Good News Bible*, op cit

75 Carmen Bernos de Gasztoid, 'The Prayer of the Lark', *Prayers from the Ark*, Macmillan, London, 1963, p. 29

76 C. S. Lewis, *The Magician's Nephew*, Penguin Books, Harmondsworth, 1963, pp. 93–5. By permission of The Bodley Head

77 Richard Baker, *The Magic of Music*, Hamish Hamilton, London, 1975, pp. 13–14

78 Herbert Brokering, 'Rhythm', *Worlds of Youth*, Concordia Publishing House, St Louis, 1967, pp. 16–17

79 James Baldwin, *Another Country*, Corgi Books, London, 1962, p. 6. By permission of Michael Joseph Ltd

80 Edward Robinson, *The Original Vision*, The Religious Experience Research Unit, Oxford, 1977, p. 90

81 John Paynter and Peter Aston, *Sound and Silence*, Cambridge University Press, Cambridge, 1970, p. 24

82 Walter de la Mare, 'Music'. Quoted from *The Complete Poems*, Faber and Faber, London, 1969, p. 199. Used by permission of the Literary Trustees of Walter de la Mare and the Society of Authors as their representative

83 Thomas Hardy, *Tess of the D'Urbervilles*, Macmillan, London, 1975, pp. 150–1

84 I Samuel 16:14–19, 23, *New English Bible*, op cit

85 Carson McCullers, *The Heart is a Lonely Hunter*, Cresset Press, London, 1943, pp. 99–101. Used by permission Cresset Press, a part of the Hutchinson Group

86 A. A. Milne, *The House at Pooh Corner*, Methuen, London, 1965, p. 79. By permission Methuen Children's Books

87 'The silver swan', anonymous, 1612

88 James Stephens, 'The Shell', *Collected Poems*, Macmillan, London, 1926, pp. 27–8. Used by permission of The Society of Authors on behalf of the copyright owner, Mrs Iris Wise

89 James Joyce, 'Chamber Music XXXV, *Chamber Music*, Jonathan Cape, London, 1907, p. 39. Used by permission of the Executors of the James Joyce Estate

90 Norman MacCaig, 'Frustrated Virtuoso', *The White Bird*, Hogarth Press, London, 1973, p. 33. Used by permission of Chatto and Windus Ltd

91 Walt Whitman, 'I hear America singing', *Leaves of Grass*, op. cit., pp. 12–13

92 Job 38:1–7, *Jerusalem Bible*, op cit

93 J. Montgomery, 'Angels from the realms of glory', in most hymn books

94 Luke 2:8–14, *Good News Bible*, op cit

95 Erik Routley, 'New songs of celebration', © 1974 by Agape, Carol Stream International copyright secured. All rights reserved. Used by permission

96 A Song of Creation, *The Alternative Service Book 1980*

97 Ephesians 5:18–20, *Revised Standard Version*

98 George Herbert, 'Let all the world in every corner sing': in Collected Editions of his poems, and in many hymn books

99 Robin Leaver, 'Music in church today', *Anglican Worship Today*, Collins, London, 1980, pp. 49–52, passim

100 Psalm 150, *Jerusalem Bible*, op cit

101 Thomas Hardy, *Under the Greenwood Tree*, Macmillan, London, 1974, pp. 48–50

102 Joseph Gelineau, *The Liturgy Today and Tomorrow*, op cit, p. 92

103 Ian Barton, 'Christmas Day Mass in a Russian Monastery – 6 January 1973', in Geoffrey Bruce and Ian Barton, *Listen! Music and Civilisation*, Cambridge University Press, London, 1978, p. 19. Used by permission

104 Thomas Merton, *The Seven Storey Mountain*, Sheldon Press, London, 1975, pp. 379–80. Used by permission

105 Harvey Cox, *Turning East*, Touchstone, New York, 1977, pp. 111–12

106 Harvey Cox, *The Seduction of the Spirit*, Touchstone, New York, 1973, pp. 156–8